THE NATURAL HISTORY OF THE EDWARDS PLATEAU

INTEGRATIVE NATURAL HISTORY SERIES

Sponsored by Texas Research

Institute for Environmental Studies,

Sam Houston State University

William I. Lutterschmidt and

Brian R. Chapman, General Editors

THE NATURAL HISTORY
OF THE EDWARDS PLATEAU

THE TEXAS HILL COUNTRY

BRIAN R. CHAPMAN AND ERIC G. BOLEN

foreword by MARGIE CRISP

TEXAS A&M UNIVERSITY PRESS

College Station

This paper meets the requirements of ANSI/NISO Z39.48–1992 (Permanence of Paper).
Binding materials have been chosen for durability.
Printed in Canada by Friesens.

♾ ♻

Library of Congress Cataloging-in-Publication Data

Names: Chapman, Brian R., author. | Bolen, Eric G., author. | Crisp,
    Margie, 1960– writer of foreword.
Title: The natural history of the Edwards Plateau: the Texas Hill Country
    / Brian R. Chapman and Eric G. Bolen; foreword by Margie Crisp.
Other titles: Integrative natural history series.
Description: First edition. | College Station: Texas A&M University
    Press, [2020] | Series: Integrative natural history series | Includes
    bibliographical references (pages 55–62) and index.
Identifiers: LCCN 2019057723 (print) | LCCN 2019057724 (ebook) |
    ISBN 9781623498597 (paperback) | ISBN 9781623498603 (ebook)
Subjects: LCSH: Natural history—Texas—Edwards Plateau. |
    Ecology—Texas—Edwards Plateau. | Texas Hill Country (Tex.)
Classification: LCC QH105.T4 C4857 2020 (print) | LCC QH105.T4 (ebook) |
    DDC 508.764—dc23
LC record available at https://lccn.loc.gov/2019057723
LC ebook record available at https://lccn.loc.gov/2019057724

To naturalists everywhere,
past, present, and future,
but especially to
ROY BEDICHEK, J. FRANK DOBIE,
AND WALTER PRESCOTT WEBB,
the three friends who saved Barton Springs.

CONTENTS

FOREWORD

Not long after I moved back to Austin in the mid-1980s, new friends and coworkers started telling me about places I had to visit. At the time, I thought it was because of my rather obvious longing for the hiking trails, whitewater rivers, and deep forests of the Appalachians I'd left behind, but now I realize that it was pride in the natural beauty of Texas that prompted them to assure me that I would love these places. In no time I had a list of must-visit parks for hiking and camping, with Enchanted Rock State Natural Area, Pedernales Falls State Park, Lost Maples State Natural Area, and Big Bend National Park topping the list. One May weekend I stuffed sleeping bag, bagels, peanut butter, canteen, coffee kit, and flashlight into a pack and drove to Enchanted Rock. The parking lot was packed with cars and I was astonished by the number of people scampering over the domes, looking like so many insects. Joining the line of hikers on one of the well-worn trails, I made it to the top of the largest pink granite dome. At first glance, I saw a passing resemblance to the mountaintop balds of North Carolina, but as I stepped carefully over the shield-like slabs of stone, I realized how profoundly different it all was. Basking in the late afternoon sun like one of the many resident lizards, I looked out over the oak woodlands surrounding the domes and at the cacti, shrubs, and grasses prying their roots into rock clefts. As the setting sun gilded the domes and set the hills ablaze, a cool breeze zipped up the granite slope and warned me that night was coming. While dusk settled in the woods, the day visitors drove away and I hiked around the base of the domes and out to the primitive camping area. I threw my sleeping bag down where I planned to watch the stars rise over the granite domes. It had been months since I'd slept without a roof; I fell asleep listening to the groans and snaps of stone cooling in the spring night, as coyotes sang the stars into the sky and rotund clouds flickered with distant lightening.

At about 2:00 a.m. I was woken by a few fat raindrops splatting on my face and sleeping bag. I pulled the nylon up over my head thinking it wouldn't last. Thirty seconds later it was as if someone had hurled a bucket of cold water over me. The rain roared down, soaking my sleeping bag through and turning my camp into a small tributary stream.

I draped my sodden sleeping bag over my head and shoulders and retrieved my gear as it floated into the brush. My flashlight flickered as water sloshed around the light. With a pop the bulb broke. I stood in the deluge and listened to thunder rumbling around me. I thought about the clumps of prickly pear I'd dodged along the path—until my friends' stories and warnings about rattlesnakes flooded into my mind. Lightning flashed and lit up the domes of Enchanted Rock and the path before me. No spines or venomous creatures for at least ten feet. Thunder boomed and I dashed a few feet. A small tree appeared in the middle of the path and embraced me with thorny limbs. I shrugged it off and waited for the next lightning strike. I returned to the trail and made it another fifteen feet. Sheets of rain sluiced over me as I waited for lightning strikes to crackle across the sky and light my way.

I have no recollection of how long it took me to walk out. What I do remember is the wild beauty of lightning-lit trees and the strange shapes of black-shadowed jumbled boulders seen through a veil of glittering rain. When I reached the parking lot, I dumped my gear on a picnic table and crawled into my car for a few cold and soggy hours of sleep. The heavy percussion of rain slowed and then stopped, waking me in the predawn darkness. I found and ate a surprisingly water-resistant bagel, jammed my belongings into the car, and started driving. I immediately got lost. Deer, raccoons, armadillos, and coyotes watched me as I wandered down one looping ranch road after another. The sun rose and a long shaft of light suddenly illuminated a sparkling profusion of wildflowers, prickly pears, and grasses blanketing the roadside. Crimsons, scarlets, butter yellows, and ultramarines highlighted viridian and jade backgrounds, with raindrops flashing off petals and leaves. I stopped the car and stood, stunned, at the spectacle of wildflowers running from the limestone road and into the distance as far as I could see. I felt washed as clean as the cloudless blue sky. In less than twenty-four hours I had witnessed some of the best—and the worst—that the Edwards Plateau offers. I was smitten.

Fortunately, most people don't have such a dramatic introduction to the Edwards Plateau's extraordinary convergence of topography, weather, and vegetation. It is, however, a region of contrasts: drought and flood, endangered species and invasive species, thorny plants and wildflower panoramas. In areas where the land has been historically misunderstood and overused, it can seem to be nothing but rocks and cedar, but as Brian R. Chapman and Eric G. Bolen describe in eloquent prose, this ecoregion encompassing the heart of Texas is so much more. In this highly readable masterwork, the authors have linked historical accounts and contemporary scholarly research to craft an enjoyable and complete vision of a complex area. Like skilled fireside raconteurs, they lead you into the story, describing the denizens—both famous and infamous—that bring the Hill Country to life, threading the story through karst, caves, caverns, granite uplifts, geological faults, and cedar breaks to create a deeply affectionate portrait of an extraordinarily diverse natural region.

As our state's population continues to grow, as cities creep farther afield each day, and as family lands are cut into smaller and smaller portions and plots, this account of the rich natural history of the Edwards Plateau will be an essential guide to those who love our state—whether they be landowners who hope to restore their corner of the Hill Country; the hikers, bird-watchers, and wildflower peepers who return year after year; or the professionals and politicians who make decisions that impact our lands and waters.

Ultimately, this book is destined for anyone who loves the canyons and windswept plateaus. And for all those who are inspired to conjure a future where springs still flow into rivers, rivers run through cypress-lined canyons, and native grasses and wildflowers grow in profusion among the limestone and granite hills of the Edwards Plateau.

MARGIE CRISP
Author of River of Contrasts: The Texas Colorado *and* The Nueces River: Río Escondido

PREFACE

This volume was excerpted from our larger statewide work, *The Natural History of Texas*, which endeavored to portray the uniqueness of the plant and animal communities in each of 11 natural regions. Predictably, the original effort produced a hefty book, which we fondly call our Texas Tome, whose coverage may lie beyond what is desired by those interested in specific areas of the state. Our editors thus proposed that a series of smaller regional books be carved from the larger volume, of which *The Natural History of the Edwards Plateau: The Texas Hill Country* is the first to appear. This selection considered the magnetic attractiveness of the region to tourists and newcomers to the state. Residents, of course, already bask in the knowledge that their land is enriched, like no other, with fields of colorful wildflowers, scenic rivers, and magnificent formations of ancient rocks. But for all, "Deep in the Heart of Texas" voices a lyrical spotlight on the Hill Country.

The Edwards Plateau is nothing if not a geological wonderland of limestone and storied outcrops of granite. The etched canyonlands lying beyond the abrupt Balcones Escarpment star on this ancient stage, with a supporting cast headed by an imposing granite dome, Enchanted Rock, and an "uplift" that is really a basin filled with rocks dating to the very dawn of life on our planet. In Mason County, fossils known as stromatolites bear the remains of primitive cyanobacteria (a.k.a. blue-green algae) that contributed to the oxygenation of Earth's atmosphere more than a half billion years ago.

The landscape is also enriched by hills thick with "cedars," the regional lingo for juniper, thousands of caves, and a grove of "lost" maples, all watered by enchanting rivers and sparkling springs. Some of the streams support native populations of Guadalupe Bass, the official freshwater fish of Texas, and many provide habitat for several species of mussels, a few of which occur nowhere else. In Texas, the cave-rich Edwards Plateau is the place to go for spelunkers as well as for millions of bats whose nightly harvests help farmers curtail insect damage. Flooded caves harbor an interesting fauna, of which the ghostly and stick-thin Texas Blind Salamander deserves mention, in part because of its endangered status. White-tailed Deer abound in the Edwards Plateau, in places reaching densities greater than anywhere else in the state or nation, and the livestock on some ranches includes big game animals from far-off lands as well as cattle. Birds, too, spice the regional fauna, including the Golden-cheeked Warbler, an endemic "specialty" that depends exclusively on the bark of Ashe Juniper for its nest materials.

In spring and early summer, fields flush with wildflowers provide a palette of color to the Edwards Plateau. Of these, bluebonnet and Texas Firewheel stand out, but many other species also paint the countryside. Given the stunning beauty of these settings, it is not hard to understand how Claudia "Lady Bird" Johnson came to champion roadside landscaping and, eventually, to establish her namesake wildflower center near Austin, the premier organization of its kind. Accordingly, we proudly include, as one of several infoboxes in the text, a brief résumé of her life, contributions, and honors.

These few words offer no more than a snapshot of the Edwards Plateau, but we hope you will find in the following pages a fuller picture of this magic land. It's all here—in the Edwards Plateau!

ACKNOWLEDGMENTS

Many persons, listed by name in the parent volume, *The Natural History of Texas*, contributed to our work, and we again thank one and all for sharing with us their time and expertise. We appreciate the additional contributions to this volume made by John Karges and Raymond C. Telfair II. Throughout our toils Sandy and Elizabeth remain steadfastly at our side, just as they always have.

The preparation of this book benefited from editorial guidance provided by the staff at Texas A&M University Press. We especially thank Shannon Davies, Emily Seyl, Stacy Eisenstark, Jay Dew, Katie Duelm, and Laurel Anderton for their efforts.

THE NATURAL HISTORY OF THE EDWARDS PLATEAU

NATURAL HISTORY
IN TEXAS
ESTABLISHING ECOLOGICAL BOUNDARIES

It may be the naturalists who save us in the end, by bringing us all back down to earth.

— ROBERT MICHAEL PYLE (2001)

A TEXTURED LANDSCAPE

Whether one travels north to south or east to west, Texas stretches for nearly 800 miles and sprawls across 267,000 square miles of the American Southwest. Besides bragging rights, such an expanse also endows Texas with what arguably represents the richest variety of ecological conditions of any state in the nation, including the "slightly" larger Alaska: rough-hewn desert, grasslands of several kinds, piney woods, coastal marshes, juniper-covered hills, and a semitropical floodplain represent a quick, yet still incomplete, look across the state's varied landscape (fig. 1). Missing from this overview are bat-filled caves, the shifting dunes at Monahans, the magnificent canyons along both the Rio Grande and the eastern escarpment of the Llano Estacado, the riparian swamps and hardwood bottoms, even a few mountains, and the coastal ribbons we call barrier islands, but also—well, you get the picture. Texas is textured by a landscape as varied as it is big.

EARLY NATURAL HISTORY IN TEXAS

Nineteenth-century naturalists recognized the uniqueness of Texas beginning with the expedition of Thomas Freeman and Peter Custis (1806) up the Red River. The latter separated Texas from the vast—and largely unknown—lands of the Louisiana Territory acquired by Thomas Jefferson. Jefferson, a president with more than a passing interest in natural history, had recently authorized the much heralded Lewis and Clark Expedition (1804–1806) and had similarly charged Freeman and Custis to explore the southern edge of the new addition to the United States. Regrettably, Freeman and Custis were turned back by the Spanish army just as their expedition entered Texas at present-day Bowie County. Had they been able to go on, the explorers might have continued upstream to the headwaters of the Red River and the majestic canyonlands on the eastern border of the High Plains—a discovery that awaited the trek of Army Captain Randolph Marcy (1812–1887) in 1852 (fig. 2). Like the Lewis and Clark Expedition, the Freeman and Custis

Expedition included no naturalists, but also like their more famous predecessors, Freeman and Custis collected numerous specimens of interest to natural history, which included a then-unknown raptor, the Mississippi Kite.

In 1820, Major Stephen H. Long (1784–1864) led an expedition to explore the headwaters of the Platte, Arkansas, and Red Rivers. His troop included a botanist, Edwin James (1797–1861), a zoologist and entomologist, Thomas Say (1787–1834), and an artist-naturalist, Titian Peale (1799–1885). After reaching Colorado, the party turned south and split, one group descending the Arkansas River and the other (with James and Peale) striking even farther south in search of the Red River. Mistakenly, the latter instead followed the Canadian River and thus unknowingly turned their topographical error into the first scientific expedition to enter Texas.

Not long afterward, John James Audubon (1785–1851) visited Texas to continue his observations and paintings for his monumental *Birds of America*. Texas did not disappoint. He wrote, "The mass of observations that we gathered [in Texas] connected with the ornithology of our country has, I think, never been surpassed." Audubon's visit, made in the spring of 1837, included stops on Galveston Island and Buffalo Bayou. For those readers familiar with the current industrial development along the Houston Ship Channel and the lower reaches of Buffalo Bayou, note Audubon's description: "This bayou is . . . bordered on both sides with a strip of woods [where] I found the Ivory-billed Woodpecker in abundance." In keeping with his routine field methods, Audubon shot several specimens of what is today generally considered an extinct species in mainland North America. Lying just beyond the riparian forest bordering the bayou were extensive coastal prairies where the artist-naturalist expressed surprise as to how well these grasslands provided a niche for Black-throated Buntings, today known as Dickcissels (fig. 3). Audubon and his son, John Woodhouse Audubon, concluded their 27-day tour by visiting with Sam Houston, then president of the newly established Republic of Texas.

Searches for a feasible route for a transcontinental railway across the vast North American interior spurred further exploration of the American West during the 1850s. One of

(*overleaf*) **Figure 1. Extensive forests—habitats not always associated with Texas—in East Texas represent just one of its many-textured landscapes. Photograph by Jonathan K. Gerland.**

Figure 2. Shaped by tributaries of the Red River, the red-hued Palo Duro Canyonlands remained uncharted until explored by Captain Marcy in 1852.

Figure 3. Extensive coastal prairies like this one in Austin County provided John James Audubon with opportunities to observe Dickcissels. Photograph by Sandra S. Chapman.

these, led by Lieutenant Amiel Whipple (1813–1863) in 1853–1854, traversed the 35th parallel along the Canadian River, which might well have been selected as the route had Whipple's math been better (much of his pathway, however, later become famous as Route 66). Whipple's expedition included scientists associated with the Smithsonian Institution, and their reports, along with those from the other railroad surveys, filled 12 huge volumes with knowledge of the American West. With the marriage of the Union Pacific and Central Pacific Railroads in 1869, the way west opened and spurred the rise of competitive routes, notably that of the Southern Pacific, whose tracks crossed the Trans-Pecos. A network of branch lines soon spread outward from these trunk lines, providing access for a growing corps of intrepid botanists, zoologists, and geologists to an ever-shrinking American frontier destined to disappear by 1890.

Meanwhile, two European naturalists, Thomas Drummond from Scotland (1793–1835) and Swiss-born Jean Louis Berlandier (1805–1851), visited Texas. Both collected plants for the most part, but also birds and other vertebrates. Drummond made two trips to North America, the second of which, begun in 1831, included the Allegheny Mountains west to St. Louis and eventually New Orleans before he landed in Texas near present-day Freeport and headed inland. He collected about 750 species of plants and 150 birds between Galveston Island and the Edwards Plateau, especially along the Brazos, Colorado, and Guadalupe Rivers. Drummond commended two flowers, Tickseed and Firewheel, as "deserving of notice for their beauty." Both are now common roadside plants, with the copper tones of Firewheel inspiring the school colors for Texas State University in San Marcos (fig. 4). Drummond also attempted to collect insects but found few, which he attributed to the "custom of burning the prairies," a practice still widely employed today to maintain native grasslands in many areas in North America. After spending nearly two years in Texas, he left for Cuba, where he died shortly after arriving. Drummond's plant collections were widely distributed across Europe, where they generated heightened interest for additional botanical work in America (fig. 4).

Berlandier began his fieldwork in Mexico,

Figure 4. Once called Firewheels (top), Indian Blankets caught the eye of Scottish naturalist Thomas Drummond, who sent plant specimens from South Texas to Europe for identification. English botanist Joseph Dalton Hooker named Drummond's Phlox (bottom) in his honor.

where he arrived in 1826, on behalf of Augustin de Candolle (1778–1841), at the time Europe's premier botanist. He served as a scientist on the Mexican Boundary Commission charged to settle the dispute with the United States over the western border of Louisiana. The expedition left Mexico City in November 1827 and entered Texas at Laredo— "a very desert place" in his words—in February of the following year. Berlandier collected along the entire route, which eventually included San Antonio, Gonzales, San Felipe, and Nacogdoches. His association with the commission effectively ended on the Trinity River in May 1828 after he was diagnosed with malaria. He was sent to Matamoros to recuperate and resided there the remainder of his life except for a brief return to Texas in 1834 to

Figure 5. Jean Louis Berlandier likely visited Presidio la Bahia at Goliad (Goliad County) in 1834.

collect near Goliad (fig. 5). Whereas Berlandier is remembered as the first botanist to collect extensively in Texas, his interests also included birds, fishes, reptiles, and insects, which he also collected and sometimes skillfully painted in watercolors. A tortoise—the smallest of its kind but with an unusually high-domed carapace—found in southern Texas and northeastern Mexico was named in his honor. Instead of burrowing like other species of tortoise, Texas (or Berlandier's) Tortoises more often clear resting places—known as pallets— under the protection of a bush or cactus; the pallets gradually deepen because of continued use for many years. The species has been protected in Texas since 1967.

Another immigrant, German-born Ferdinand J. Lindheimer (1801–1879), regarded by some as

the "Father of Texas Botany," fought in the Texas Revolution and subsequently collected plants for two prominent botanists, Asa Gray (1810–1888) at Harvard University and Georg Engelmann (1809– 1884) of St. Louis. He collected extensively in the area around Fredericksburg and New Braunfels, but also in the bottomlands of the Brazos and Guadalupe Rivers, Galveston Island, and Matagorda Bay (fig. 6). Unlike others collectors, who were often members of larger parties, Lindheimer traveled alone in a two-wheeled Mexican cart pulled by a pony. His career as an active botanist and collector for Gray and Engelmann ended in 1852, when he began editing a German-language newspaper in New Braunfels. Nonetheless, many of Lindheimer's specimens, some of which represented new species, ended up in collections throughout the world and

**Figure 6.
Ferdinand J.
Lindheimer
traveled by pony-
drawn cart to
collect plants
in bottomland
habitats like
this near the
Guadalupe River.
Photograph by
Paige A. Najvar.**

thereby established the richness of the Texas flora for botanists everywhere.

A large number of mostly amateur ornithologists dominate the cast of late-nineteenth-century naturalists in Texas—not surprising, given that its avifauna is the largest of any in the United States, leading California by about 80 species. The current list for Texas includes 639 species of birds and today boasts its own volume in the famed series of Peterson field guides (fig. 7). By the 1880s, at least 50 men and 2 women in Texas were actively engaged in some form of ornithology, often with a focus on collecting eggs, nests, or the birds themselves, but also compiling lists of species for counties or other specified areas. The interests of some included selling specimens to collectors elsewhere, but many specimens also ended up in museums in the United States and in foreign lands. Sixteen of the group were born outside the United States, and nine were native Texans. They resided in all regions of the state except for the High Plains and Trans-Pecos, and many added to the growing fund of ornithological knowledge with formal publication of their observations. Space limitations permit mention of only a few of these pioneering

naturalists. Among these are Harry Y. Benedict (1869–1937), an egg collector who later became president of the University of Texas; English-born Henry P. Attwater (1854–1931), collector of the type specimen for a subspecies of Greater Prairie-Chicken named in his honor; another Englishman, rancher Howard G. Lacey (1856–1929), who published a list of birds for the area near Kerrville; and a farmer from Corpus Christi, John M. Priour (1848–1931), who for four decades worked as a guide and collector for a number of prominent eastern ornithologists.

In terms of natural history, the second half of the nineteenth century corresponds to the Golden Age of Paleontology, in which Texas provided key sites for many discoveries. In 1877, Edward Drinker Cope (1840–1897), one side of the "Bone Wars" with Othniel C. Marsh (1831–1899) of Yale University, discovered a trove of fossils in the Permian Red Beds of north-central Texas (Baylor and surrounding counties). Cope, associated with the Philadelphia Academy of Natural Sciences, excavated thousands of fossils highlighting a critical point in evolution—the origins and dominance of terrestrial quadrupeds that mark the beginnings

Figure 7. Populations of many species, including Whooping Cranes (above) and White-winged Doves (left), have declined significantly since the late 1880s. Photographs by Terri Tipping (above) and J. Byron Stone (left).

fossils. Marsh countered Cope with discoveries of his own fossils, some at the same locations, in what proved to be a competition employing shady methods, including sabotage, and attacks in their respective publications. In time, the reputations—and fortunes—of both men suffered, but their work nonetheless produced significant contributions, including huge collections of unexamined fossils that provided research opportunities for the next generation of paleontologists. *Copeia,* the journal of the American Society of Ichthyologists and Herpetologists, first published in 1913, honors Cope and his work. Texas has been the site of extensive paleontological work involving several other well-known scientists and important discoveries of both vertebrate and invertebrate animals. However, here it will suffice to mention only the discovery of dinosaur tracks in the Cretaceous strata in the bed of the Paluxy River near Glen Rose (Somervell County) early in the twentieth century, now the site of a state park. Since then, tracks have also been discovered at additional sites in the region (fig 8).

Final mention goes to John K. Strecker (1875–

of land-based ecosystems and the initiation of terrestrial food chains. *Dimetrodon,* a mammal-like reptile outfitted with a large finlike sail on its back, was the apex predator of its time and preyed on a community dominated by amphibians. Cope later discovered other deposits, notably the Clarendon Beds (Upper Miocene and Lower Pliocene in Donley County) and the Blanco Beds (late Pliocene in Blanco County), both rich in mammalian

Figure 8. Two main types of dinosaur tracks appear in the rocky bed of the Paluxy River at Dinosaur Valley State Park. The stumpy feet of sauropods—huge herbivores that lumbered on four pillar-like legs—show little indication of toes. The three-toed tracks of theropods—fast-moving bipedal predators—also appear in the rock. Both types of dinosaurs followed the same muddy route; the footprints do not necessarily indicate a clash between predator and potential prey. Photograph by Glen Kuban.

Figure 9. Strecker's Chorus Frog was named to honor Texas naturalist John K. Strecker. Photograph by Suzanne L. Collins.

1933), whose life's work may justify the title "Father of Texas Natural History." By horse and buggy, he traveled widely in Texas, collecting animals of many kinds but especially reptiles, amphibians, birds, and mollusks, fulfilling his duties as the museum curator (and librarian) at Baylor University— accomplishments he earned with no more than a grade-school education. In 1940, the museum, now part of a larger museum complex at Baylor, was renamed in his honor. In all, he published 111 papers based on his fieldwork, plus many popular articles. His studies of amphibians and reptiles

established him as a recognized authority in herpetology. Similarly, a monograph dealing with freshwater mussels and another on aquatic and land snails likewise earned the commendation of malacologists; both papers remain widely cited. For fieldwork, he always dressed in a tie, believing that this formality convinced farmers and ranchers that he was worthy of access to their property. Strecker represented the last of the "old-time" naturalists in Texas—those who gained broad self-taught knowledge about wild things and their place in nature. Strecker's Chorus Frog, named in his honor, occurs in a broad band across eastern Texas, Oklahoma, and barely into southern Kansas; isolated populations also occur in Illinois, Missouri, and Arkansas (fig. 9). Unlike most other burrowing frogs and toads, this species digs using its stout front limbs and enters burrows headfirst.

The early era of natural history in Texas faded in the decade spanning the turn of the nineteenth century and the beginning of the twentieth, when a modern cadre of naturalists began fieldwork in the state. Notable among these were mammalogist Vernon O. Bailey (infobox 1) and ornithologist Harry C. Oberholser (infobox 2), who launched formal investigations of the state's biological resources on behalf of the Bureau of Biological Survey. Unlike the railroad surveys, in which natural history was a secondary interest and of relatively limited geographical coverage, fieldwork in the new era became the primary mission, whose sole purpose was cataloging plants and animals in *all* parts of Texas. This change in scope included similar work ongoing in other states and more or

INFOBOX 1. VERNON O. BAILEY
Field Naturalist of the Old School (1864–1942)

Few biologists can match the field experience acquired by Vernon Bailey. Although born in Michigan, Vernon and his pioneer family settled in Minnesota on what was then still a largely untrammeled frontier. His parents provided his early schooling, followed by somewhat more formal training when the community eventually built a schoolhouse. Bailey farmed for a few years after finishing his rustic education but later briefly attended the University of Michigan and, still later, what is now George Washington University.

Meanwhile, in Washington, DC, a fledgling government agency was developing that would later become the Bureau of Biological Survey, the federal agency whose mission focused on what is now known as wildlife ecology and management. While in Minnesota, Bailey taught himself taxidermy and amassed a collection of specimens, some of which—particularly shrews—he could not identify. Accordingly, he contacted the agency's director, C. Hart Merriam, who quickly established an appreciation for the young man's skills and began buying Bailey's specimens for the national collection in Washington. Merriam also advised Bailey on ways to measure, label, and catalog his specimens. In 1887, Merriam hired Bailey as a field agent and ten years later appointed him as the agency's Chief Field Naturalist—the first and only person to hold that title—which he retained until his retirement from government service in 1933.

Bailey spent much of his career on fieldwork. The locations covered a broad swath of environments, from the northern forests and mountains of Glacier National Park in Montana to the dark recesses of Carlsbad Caverns in New Mexico. His fieldwork, which centered on mammals and was supplemented by observations of birds, reptiles, and plants, became the basis for 244 published works. His trapping efforts produced some 13,000 specimens of mammals for the bureau's collection; these also provided both Bailey and Merriam with material they used to designate a wealth of new species and subspecies. Both men developed a deep interest in taxonomy, and both were regarded as "splitters" (they often divided species into subspecies) when dealing with variations in pelage or skeletal measurements. Although several of their designations have not survived the rigor of modern scrutiny, a species of pocket mouse and a subspecies of Bobcat that Merriam named after Bailey remain unchanged.

In 1889, after earlier rejecting Merriam's wishes on the matter, Bailey made the first of seven trips to Texas. His initial fieldwork focused on the Trans-Pecos, but he later covered the entire state. Six of Bailey's larger works appeared in the North American Fauna series. One of these, published in 1905, bears the title *Biological Survey of Texas.* The monograph reports at length on the state's mammalian fauna, supplemented by lists of reptiles and birds he observed. He separated the plants and animals in the survey on the basis of "life zones"—ecological units proposed by Merriam based on biological communities that vary in relation to latitude (see main text). Among other observations, Bailey estimated that no fewer than 400 million Black-tailed Prairie Dogs occupied the huge colony stretching along the eastern edge of the Llano Estacado from San Angelo to Clarendon. He also noted when and where the last American Bison were killed in Texas. His survey remains a useful baseline for comparison with the current status of wildlife in Texas; reprinted editions of the bulletin are still published.

Bailey married Merriam's sister, Florence, herself an accomplished naturalist with a special interest in ornithology and the author of several books, including an acclaimed field guide. She accompanied her husband on his trip to South Texas, traveling by bumpy wagon throughout the brushy terrain between Corpus Christi and the border with Mexico.

In 1919, Bailey helped found the American Society of Mammalogists and later (1933–1935) served as its president. In the first issue of the society's journal, Bailey published a description of a new subspecies of beaver—*Castor canadensis missouriensis*—still recognized in mammalian taxonomy. He was also a member of ornithological societies and other professional groups concerned with the conservation of natural resources. Bailey remained active after retiring, including nature photography, lecturing, and even fieldwork. He also continued designing and perfecting live traps, particularly those developed to catch beaver alive and unhurt in order to restock areas where they had been extirpated—work recognized with prizes from the American Humane Association. At the time of his death, Bailey was planning another field trip to Texas in association with the US Fish and Wildlife Service. He died as he had lived: a field man at heart.

INFOBOX 2. *THE BIRD LIFE OF TEXAS*
The Life's Work of Harry C. Oberholser
(1870–1963)

Few biologists have devoted a career-long study to the birds of a state, especially when living elsewhere. Among these, Harry C. Oberholser comes close to standing alone in his dedication, in this case to the avifauna of Texas, which he began studying in 1900 and continued to study until his death 63 years later. Born in Brooklyn, New York, Oberholser briefly studied at Columbia University but left because of poor health. He then worked in his father's dry-goods store in Ohio, where he compiled a list of birds for Wayne County that was later published by the state's Agricultural Experiment Station—the first of nearly 900 publications, including a book about the birds of Louisiana. In 1895, he accepted a position in Washington, DC, as ornithological clerk for the Division of Economic Ornithology in the Department of Agriculture, precursor to the US Fish and Wildlife Service in the Department of the Interior. He resumed his education and in 1916 earned a PhD from George Washington University.

Oberholser undertook a variety of duties while in government service, but these always concerned birds. In 1900, the then 30-year-old Oberholser landed in Texas at Port Lavaca to begin fieldwork. Previously, field agents had collected specimens in parts of the state, but Oberholser was charged to expand the project statewide with his own fieldwork, supplemented by information gleaned from both local naturalists and published literature. This was the first of three trips, one of which (in 1901) included traveling with Vernon Bailey (infobox 1) and Louis Agassiz Fuertes (1874–1927), whose extraordinary artwork would appear decades later in pages of Oberholser's life's work—a manuscript initiated in his reports of these trips.

In 1928, Oberholser organized a census that continues today as the Winter Waterfowl Survey, an important tool in managing ducks, geese, and swans in each of North America's four flyways. He also successfully advocated that bird banding become a federal program coordinated and managed by the Bureau of Biological Survey. When time permitted, he served as a professor of zoology at both the Biltmore Forest summer school in North Carolina and the American University graduate school in Washington, DC. He was a member of 40 scientific and conservation societies, many in other countries.

Notably, he was a charter and honorary member of the Texas Ornithological Society.

In 1941, after a tenure of 46 years, he retired as Senior Biologist, having benefited from a presidential order that granted an additional year of service beyond the mandatory retirement age (70) to further his work on Texas birds. He then spent the next six years in Ohio as curator of ornithology at the Cleveland Museum of Natural History, retiring a second and final time in 1947.

Throughout his career, Oberholser maintained an interest in avian taxonomy and examined thousands of study skins for variations in plumage and morphology. Even the slightest differences between geographical populations of the same species caught his attention, and these often became the basis for declaring and naming subspecies. Oberholser soon earned a reputation as a "splitter," about which many of his colleagues did not always speak approvingly. In all, he named 11 new families and subfamilies, 99 genera and subgenera, and 560 species and subspecies of birds worldwide. He also identified thousands of birds sent to Washington by other agencies, museums, and private collectors. His detailed knowledge of feathers and avian anatomy also led to numerous appearances in court, where such evidence helped prosecute violators of federal wildlife laws.

Until his death in 1963, Oberholser continually added new information to a project—a comprehensive study of Texas birds—that had begun with a field trip across the state more than six decades earlier. In the end, the typed manuscript reached nearly 12,000 pages and three million words. A work of such length understandably overpowered potential publishers, and publication of his epic treatise indeed experienced several false starts. The original manuscript included four sections: the history of ornithological studies in Texas dating to 1828; species accounts, detailing the distribution of each species and subspecies; a gazetteer listing places where birds were observed or collected; and a 572-page bibliography. Much of this material was heavily edited, supplemented, or deleted in full (e.g., the gazetteer) in readying the original manuscript for publication.

Thus, only after his death and with considerable editorial work did Oberholser's epic finally appear (in 1974) in print, but even shortened, *The Bird Life of Texas* stands as a monument to a long and fruitful career in ornithology. For scholars, an unedited copy of Oberholser's original manuscript is available for study at the Briscoe Center for American History at the University of Texas at Austin.

less coincided with efforts to develop systems to classify nature on a broad geographical scale.

ESTABLISHING ECOLOGICAL BOUNDARIES

Efforts designed to fit the landscapes of North America into discernible units were founded on taxonomic studies that, in turn, revealed distributional patterns. Plants and animals are not randomly distributed but instead show certain affinities, particularly those associated with climate and elevation and the vegetation they produce, but also with soils and the subtle variations in those conditions collectively known as "habitat." Some species, of course, have adapted to a wider range of conditions than others—White-tailed Deer, for example—yet others are far more restricted and become indicators of a relatively narrow set of ecological circumstances. Nonetheless, fine tuned or not, plants and animals sort out into ecological assemblages—the bricks of biogeography.

Biomes represent the largest units of biogeography in which similar vegetation, regardless of its location, is lumped together. Hence, the Great Plains of North America, the steppes of Russia, the pampas of Argentina, and the veldt of Africa are united in the Grassland Biome. Within North America itself, the grassland biome encompasses the Palouse Prairie in the northwest, the annual grasslands in California, the coastal prairies of Texas, and, of course, the Great Plains, each distinctive but nonetheless representing a single biome. Additional biomes in North America include Eastern Deciduous Forest, Desert, and Boreal Forest, among others.

In the late 1800s, C. Hart Merriam (1855–1942), then the head of what was soon to become the Bureau of Biological Survey and eventually today's US Fish and Wildlife Service, tweezed out smaller units he called life zones. His motives were primarily economic, as he hoped that the boundaries between life zones would guide agricultural development and lessen the need for costly attempts by trial and error. Merriam based his life-zone concept on the belts of vegetation, sorted by elevation, found in the San Francisco Mountains and surrounding areas near Flagstaff, Arizona. He recognized six zones and, after

adding two more to represent regions east of the Mississippi River, extrapolated and expanded these to cover all of North America. The Hudsonian Zone, for example, included the coniferous forests of northern Canada as well as those just below timberline on mountains farther south that were widely separated from each other by other zones. In so doing, Merriam relied almost entirely on temperature to explain the limits of plant and animal distributions—isotherms delineated the boundaries of each life zone in his system.

Whereas the life-zone concept initially gained general acceptance—it worked particularly well in the western regions—other biologists soon challenged Merriam's reliance on temperature as the primary factor controlling plant and animal distributions. Precipitation-evaporation ratios, for example, seemed as important as temperature in influencing the distribution of plants. In time, Merriam's life zones fell into disuse, in part because too many distinctive communities—among them sagebrush in the Great Basin and scrub oak chaparral in Arizona—were united within a single unit, in this case what he called the Upper Sonoran. For Texas, the same limitation—reliance on temperature at the expense of other ecological influences—united the semitropical Lower Rio Grande Valley with the eastern Panhandle and the arid Trans-Pecos, hardly a discriminating combination (fig. 10). Moreover, his isotherms considered only summer temperatures above 43°F, thereby ignoring the limitations posed by cold winters (in fact, because of a misunderstanding, the Weather Bureau provided Merriam with threshold values based on 32°F, thus invalidating the isotherms presented in his work). Still, Merriam deserves credit for attempting to explain the distribution of North American biota and for stimulating further interest in biogeography. But if his reliance on temperature made his calculations faulty, his descriptions of vegetation were not, and for many years they remained a useful resource for field biologists in the western United States.

In 1943, ecologist Lee Dice (1887–1977) presented descriptions and maps of 29 sizable areas called biotic provinces; he did not coin the term but refined the concept and applied it to all of North America. Each area is characterized not only by the

Figure 10.
The serrated
beauty of the
Trans-Pecos
region reflects the
complex origins
of a habitat vastly
different from
that of the Texas
Panhandle or
Lower Rio Grande
Valley.

dominant or climax vegetation but also by soil type, topographical features, biota, climate, and, when appropriate, unusual vegetation. The boundaries, however, do not reflect rigid geographic limits of species but instead portray the "distinctness and distributions of the various ecologic associations." Unlike the components forming a biome, which may occur in two or more widely separated regions, biotic provinces represent a single, continuous geographical entity unlike any other. Moreover, the demarcation between adjacent biotic provinces is certainly not a well-defined "line in the sand." Instead, one generally intergrades into another in zones known as ecotones that, as implied, blend adjacent ecological units with a mixture of species representing each. Interestingly, Dice often named his biotic provinces for prominent cultural entities. Hence, the Eskimoan Biotic Province coincides with the tundra of the far north, and Apachian designates the high grassy plains and mountains in a continuous area of southeastern Arizona, southeastern New Mexico, and parts of adjacent Mexico.

In 1950, biologist W. Frank Blair (a Dice student; see infobox 3) described the biotic provinces of Texas by associating the distribution of terrestrial vertebrates—excluding birds—with the dominant types of vegetation. In doing so, he started with the biotic provinces established by Dice, although he worked on a different scale—statewide rather than continental—and therefore benefited from a closer look at the plant and animal assemblages as well as soil types on which to map these units in Texas. Significantly, his analysis replaced Dice's Comanchian Biotic Province with a new and somewhat smaller unit, the Balconian Biotic Province, thereby highlighting the distinctive ecology of the Edwards Plateau. Both Dice and Blair recognized the Texas Biotic Province despite the highly varied vegetation within its boundaries, although Blair acknowledged it as an "unsatisfactory" designation. In Texas, this unit extends north to south from the Red River to the marshes on the Gulf Coast, a wide swath that includes the Cross Timbers and Blackland Prairies. The Texas Biotic Province indeed represents a transitional region—itself a large ecotone— between the humid forests of eastern Texas and the semiarid grasslands to the west. Later, closer looks at certain groups revealed further inconsistencies with the boundaries designated by both Dice and Blair. The amphibian and reptilian fauna in the Guadalupe Mountains, for example, matches better with the Chihuahuan than with the Navahonian

INFOBOX 3. W. FRANK BLAIR
Herpetologist and Evolutionary Biologist
(1912–1985)

A native Texan, W. Frank Blair earned a PhD in zoology in 1938 at the University of Michigan, where he remained for four years as a research associate. His studies during this period included those concerned with the home ranges of small mammals and the adaptations of pelage color to match the dark (lava) and light soils in the White Sands area of New Mexico. His doctoral work was supervised by Lee R. Dice (1887–1977), who championed the use of biotic provinces to designate ecological units in North America. Blair joined the Army Air Corps in 1942. After the war, he returned to Michigan but soon accepted an appointment to the University of Texas and began what was to be a distinguished career that continued until his retirement in 1982. Blair served as the first director of the university's Brackenridge Field Laboratory, which is dedicated to studies of biodiversity, natural history, and ecosystem changes.

Blair's academic life centered on herpetology. His particular focus on the phylogeny of toads established him as one of the world's authorities in the field of evolutionary biology. He organized summer field courses to study the biota in several regions of Texas, including Black Gap in the Big Bend area, the Glass Mountains in the Trans-Pecos, and the Canadian River Breaks in the Panhandle, among others. In keeping with his mentor's concepts of ecological classifications, Blair published *The Biotic Provinces of Texas* in 1950. Blair's early interest in mammals expanded to include the full range of vertebrates and led to publication (with coauthors) of *Vertebrates of the United States*, a landmark contribution and a standard reference for a generation of biologists. Another publication, *Evolution of the Genus* Bufo, met with wide acclaim as a seminal work of its genre.

After arriving in Austin, Blair and his wife moved into a home on land they maintained as a nature preserve. Affectionately known as their "ten acres," the site also provided Blair with an after-hours study area where he investigated the dynamics of the resident lizard population—his analysis produced another masterpiece, *The Rusty Lizard, a Population Study*. He bequeathed his beloved "ten acres" to the Travis Audubon Society, which operates the site—formally known as Blair Woods—as a natural preserve for ecological studies.

Blair believed that the mating calls of frogs were an important means of mate selection. To study these relationships, he and his students used tape recorders to capture the calls of frogs breeding in various areas, including those where the ranges of two related species overlapped. This research revealed that the calls varied geographically and played a role in maintaining reproductive isolation where similar species overlapped; the term "isolating mechanism" emerged from this and related work.

Blair's career is highlighted by service as president of the American Institute of Biological Sciences, the Ecological Society of America, the Society for the Study of Evolution, and the Texas Herpetological Society. He was a founder and guiding light, as well as president, of the Southwestern Association of Naturalists. He was active in the International Biological Program (IBP), which investigated the world's ecosystems, and served as the chair of the program's United States National Committee. Because of his contributions to IBP, Blair received the Joseph Priestley Award for 1977. More than 160 publications bear his name.

Biotic Province. In all, Blair recognized seven biotic provinces in Texas, but only the Balconian lies exclusively in the state.

Nearly two decades later, botanist Frank W. Gould (infobox 4) noted that a less theoretical, more workable, and somewhat narrower system would better serve the needs of ecologists, including those concerned with practical matters such as range management. He thus recognized "vegetational areas" based on topographical, climatic, and edaphic (soil) factors and the similarities of plant communities they produced, with each area assigned commonly used local names (fig. 11). His designations were closely aligned with the "natural geographic divisions" delineated nearly 40 years earlier by William T. Carter and included, among others, units named Cross Timbers, Edwards Plateau, High Plains, and Trans-Pecos Mountains and Basins that gained wide acceptance among laypersons, amateur naturalists, and professional biologists alike.

Newer techniques, primarily aerial mensuration and reconnaissance, allowed considerable refinement of Gould's approach. This system

INFOBOX 4. FRANK W. GOULD
Botanist (1913–1981)

Born in North Dakota, Frank W. Gould spent most of his youth elsewhere, notably in DeKalb, Illinois, where his father served as head of the geography department at Northern Illinois University. Gould stayed at home and earned his undergraduate degree at the same school. His collegiate career continued with an MS from the University of Wisconsin–Madison, where he surveyed the prairie communities remaining in Dane County. By 1941, he had finished a PhD in botany at the University of California, Berkeley, completing a taxonomic study of lilies in the genus *Camassia*. During this period, Gould also began what was to become a career focused on agrostology, the study of grasses.

In 1944, after two short teaching assignments in Utah and California, Gould assumed curatorial duties for the herbarium at the University of Arizona. Five years later, he left to become the curator of the Tracy Herbarium at Texas A&M University in College Station—his last position until his retirement in 1979. By that time—and because of Gould's diligence—the Tracy Herbarium had gained recognition as one of the most respected facilities of its kind in the United States. Throughout his career, Gould regularly acquired funding from the National Science Foundation to support his grass research and deftly used some of the money to further develop the herbarium. Today, the Tracy Herbarium houses more than 300,000 specimens, of which about 70,000 are grasses, including many that Gould collected and named (i.e., type specimens). He concurrently held a professorship in the Department of Range Science and was later awarded the title of Distinguished Professor in the same department. In keeping with advancing technology, Gould supplemented the traditional methods of taxonomy with more sophisticated cellular techniques. His memberships included the American Society of Plant Taxonomists, the Botanical Society of America, and the Society for Range Management.

As the curator of a herbarium, Gould worked professionally with plants of many kinds, but grasses remained at the center of his personal interest in plant taxonomy. His work took him to lands as diverse as Costa Rica, Sri Lanka, Brazil, and England, among others. Gould produced some 80 publications, including monographs describing the grasses of, respectively, Texas, the southwestern United States, the Coastal Bend of Texas, and Baja California (the latter work published posthumously), as well as a critically acclaimed textbook, *Grass Systematics*. At the time of his death, he had completed much of the research and some of the writing for another major work, *The Grasses of Mexico*.

Of particular relevance, we highlight *Texas Plants: A Checklist and Ecological Summary*, a work Gould revised in 1969—a publication that provides the framework for our coverage of the state's major vegetational areas. His designations—Trans-Pecos and Piney Woods, for example—closely follow those widely used by naturalists of all stripes as well as by the lay public, all of whom we include in the target audience for this book. Gould, of course, did not coin these names, but his work did much to incorporate them into the lexicon of science.

---

divided Texas into 12 large and 56 smaller ecoregions, which surely served many uses, but not necessarily those of natural history. Among other refinements, the newer system split off a small area of the Trans-Pecos to recognize the uniqueness of the Guadalupe Mountains, whereas many of the boundaries for the other ecoregions remained much as they were in Gould's work. Regrettably, at least from our standpoint, the refinements also included name changes that no longer reflected local usage or much originality. Thus, Coastal Prairies and Marshes morphed into Western Gulf Coastal Plains, and the wonderful Piney Woods lost its luster as the South Central Plains. For us, and especially for our readers, we believe Gould's designations best serve the cause of natural history and therefore guide our presentation accordingly, albeit occasionally tempered with the additional clarity of newer work. But whatever the scale, units, and titles may be, one overarching fact remains—Texas presents a wonderland of biodiversity worth our notice.

THE STATE OF NATURAL HISTORY

Natural history, as often perceived by others, diminished into an unfashionable profession in the latter half of the last century. This slide was pushed by emerging demands for the products of chemistry and physics—the so-called hard

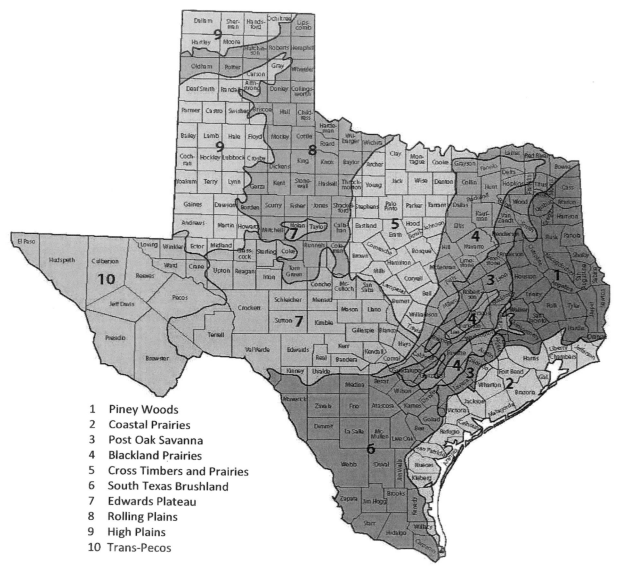

1   Piney Woods
2   Coastal Prairies
3   Post Oak Savanna
4   Blackland Prairies
5   Cross Timbers and Prairies
6   South Texas Brushland
7   Edwards Plateau
8   Rolling Plains
9   High Plains
10 Trans-Pecos

Figure 11. Map delineating the natural regions of Texas. Modified from *Illustrated Flora of East Texas* (Diggs et al. 2006); used with permission of the Botanical Research Institute of Texas.

sciences—associated with World War II and the Cold War that immediately followed. Sputnik, launched in 1957, added mathematics and microtechnology to the mix, spurring purely quantitative approaches to science, while at the same time casting an air of "soft" subjectivity on studies of wild nature. In this view, natural history represented an art, not a science, and a relic from the Victorian era of butterfly collections and cabinets filled with minerals.

Moreover, a world focused on microchips and molecular biology has largely captured the limelight for students with an interest in science,

fueled at universities by the lure of large research grants and steady promotions for its faculty who secure such funding. For budding biologists, the bandwagon shifted from outdoor to indoor studies—that is, into the cell and molecule and out of the marsh, prairie, and forest.

Meanwhile, cities and suburbs grew rapidly, severing large segments of the population from day-to-day ties with all but a well-paved landscape. Children now succumb to a world of video screens—electronic babysitters—as part of a lifestyle that often excludes treks through woods and fields or even to a park where some semblance of nature might stimulate their curiosity about the natural world. For many, any contact with nature may be solely by push button or plastic mouse.

An important component of natural history has been, and remains, the contributions of so-called amateurs—a term literally meaning "one who loves" but now corrupted to characterize someone with limited formal training in either botany or zoology. Such denigration is absurd. Amateurs, including Audubon, Strecker, and numerous physicians and army officers, who often were engineers, once formed the backbone of natural history. And they continue to make important observations. For more than a century, an annual Christmas census sponsored by the National Audubon Society and conducted largely by amateur birders has revealed trends in the distributions and populations of wild birds. Astronomy offers a useful analogy. Citizens armed with their own telescopes regularly discover a number of heavenly bodies—including comets and stray asteroids—which facilitates the work of professional astronomers tucked away in observatories. Thankfully, amateur naturalists remain actively engaged in outdoor activities, including physical as well as observational contributions, such as replanting storm-damaged dunes, serving as docents at nature centers, and assisting with prescribed burns. In contrast, however, the continued presence of an academic component in the modern corps of naturalists seems less assured.

Unfortunately, many universities have disposed of valuable plant and animal collections once used for both instruction and research. To illustrate, university collections often included bird eggs collected prior to World War II that enabled comparisons of the thickness of their shells with eggs laid during the DDT era that followed the war. These analyses documented that postwar eggshells were so thinned by pesticides that few could hatch—a discovery that provided the "smoking gun" leading to the banning of harmful agricultural chemicals. Not incidentally, many of these eggs were originally collected by dedicated amateurs known as oologists, including Texan Roy W. Quillin (1894–1974). Additionally, some universities no longer support field trips, but even more harmful is that

retiring professors representing disciplines directly related to natural history may not be replaced by those with similar academic interests. A laboratory specialist too often replaces a naturalist on the faculty. These events trigger a downward spiral: with fewer of these openings available, fewer students will prepare themselves for academic careers associated with natural history, which then slowly withers for want of both faculty and students.

Still, growing concerns about biodiversity and the health of ecosystems have somewhat checked this trend. The good news is the birth of conservation biology, a discipline dedicated to saving and restoring species and communities threatened—or worse, pushed to near extinction—by what are mostly anthropogenic agents. In response, state and federal agencies now seek college graduates—perhaps best thought of as "scientific naturalists"—equipped to deal with troubled populations of nongame species, including insects, mollusks, and amphibians and other groups often overlooked in the past, as replacements for their retirees. Moreover, new realms of life have been unveiled in environments as diverse as tree canopies and ocean vents, and these, too, require the attention of naturalists. Estimates suggest that less than a tenth of the world's species have been discovered and described—perhaps 100,000 to 400,000 in the United States alone—and the ecological role of many already discovered remains unknown.

Employment opportunities to meet these needs extend into a wide range of departments, including transportation, forestry, the military, and parks as well as wildlife management. Additionally, nongovernmental organizations— NGOs, in bureaucratic lingo—offer a growing job market for college-trained naturalists, among them the National Audubon Society, The Nature Conservancy, Sierra Club, National Wildlife Federation, and many others. All told, these opportunities require appropriate academic training, for which plant and animal taxonomy remains a common core—and a responsibility not to be shunned by universities enamored solely by molecules and test tubes.

EDWARDS PLATEAU
THE TEXAS HILL COUNTRY

*Since well over a century ago, the region has
been a sort of reference point for natives of other
parts of the state, and mention of it usually brings
smiles and nods.*

— JOHN GRAVES (2003)

Edwards Plateau

Rolling highlands separating broad valleys characterize much of the Edwards Plateau, a slightly elevated region covering approximately 24 million acres in the west-central portion of Texas. The boundaries of the somewhat oblong plateau are defined primarily by the underlying geology—horizontal layers of Cretaceous-age limestone covered by shallow calcareous soils. Deep beneath the strata lies the Edwards Aquifer, an enormous underground reservoir that feeds many crystal-clear springs (fig. 12). The plateau slopes gently from about 600 feet above sea level on the eastern edge to about 3,000 feet in the central and western regions.

The Pecos River Canyon delineates the western margin of the Edwards Plateau, but the northeastern and northwestern portions intergrade without noticeable geological demarcation into biotic associations typical of the Cross Timbers and Prairies and Southern High Plains, respectively. Only the western areas of the Edwards Plateau, where broad expanses of relatively flat uplands are dissected by shallow, gently sloping valleys, represent a true plateau. A small outlier—designated the "Callahan Divide"—is separated from the central plateau by river valleys and wide lowlands to occupy a northern fragment extending eastward from Coke and Nolan Counties to Callahan County in the middle of the state.

Sweeping in a wide arc for nearly 200 miles, a distinct change in topography defines the southern and southeastern edges of the Edwards Plateau. Along this margin, the Balcones Escarpment follows the Balcones Fault Zone, an older geologic feature rising abruptly more than 300 feet higher than the South Texas Brushland to the south and the Blackland Prairies to the east. The southernmost expanse of the plateau adjacent to the escarpment—affectionately known as the "Texas Hill Country"—is incised by numerous picturesque river canyons and steep ascents creating an undulating, wooded landscape

(*overleaf*) **Figure 12. Cold, clear water flows from Dolan Springs (Val Verde County). Photograph by Paige A. Najvar.**

composed of hills or low mountains instead of a tableland. An older geologic province, known variously as the Llano Uplift, Granitic Central Basin, or Central Mineral Region, is exposed in a comparatively small area of about 2,300 square miles along the northern margin of the Edwards Plateau. Surrounded by layers of younger Cretaceous limestones, Llano Uplift bedrock consists mostly of granitic and metamorphic rocks more than a billion years old.

Although much of the plateau is relatively flat, the region is most well known for its scenic network of crystal-clear, spring-fed streams and rivers traversing canyons cut through the layers of limestone and exposures of granite. In undisturbed areas, scattered clumps of low trees interrupt the grassy savanna. After spring rains, bluebonnets, Texas Paintbrushes, Indian Blankets, and other colorful wildflowers decorate winding Hill Country roadsides with beautiful vistas unlike any found elsewhere in the state (infobox 5).

STRUCTURE AND CLIMATE
GEOCHRONOLOGY AND STRUCTURE
The oldest rocks on the Edwards Plateau occur in the Llano Uplift area. Originally intruded as molten magma deep in the Earth's crust around 1.1 billion years ago, the well-known pink granites—known as Town Mountain Granite—in the Llano Uplift solidified underneath layers of rock. In the late Cambrian, seas inundated large parts of the continent, resulting in deposition of marine sedimentary strata—sandstones, shales, and limestones—layered directly atop the ancient rocks. Consequently, the granite reposed underground for 200 million years.

During the Permian Period, a tectonic event uplifted the region and subsequent erosion exposed the granite. When shallow continental seas periodically covered exposed surfaces of the ancient rocks beginning about 100 mya, widespread sediment deposition produced the shale and limestone layers that now characterize the entire Edwards Plateau. Evidence from across the plateau shows that the limestones were deposited in shallow tropical waters—bivalve, gastropod, and echinoderm fossils abound in some areas, reef deposits occur in others, and dinosaur footprints

INFOBOX 5. TEXAS WILDFLOWERS
Lady Bird's Legacy

In early spring, roadsides in the Hill Country and elsewhere in Texas present an eye-popping tapestry alive with a palette of vibrant colors—wildflowers have again renewed their timeless cycle across the landscape. Texas Paintbrushes and Texas Bluebonnets are among the first to weave color into the waysides browned by winter, but these soon give way to a dazzling yellow coverlet of Coreopsis. Still later, the warm and softer hues of Indian Blanket interlaced with the cool blue aura of Cornflowers and Spiderworts herald the end of another growing season. The blooms, coupled with the interplay of light and topography, easily enthrall even the most jaded traveler. The display represents a lasting legacy of a remarkable advocate for nature and the beautification of the nation's highways—Claudia Alta "Lady Bird" Taylor Johnson (1912–2007).

Shortly after her birth in Karnack, Texas, baby Claudia attracted the attention of a nurse who famously noted she was as "purty as a ladybird," thus giving rise to the nickname that would forever identify her and her good works. A shy girl during her childhood, Lady Bird spent much of her time fishing, swimming, and wandering in the forests and bayous near her home in East Texas, where she developed a deep appreciation for nature. After graduating from the University of Texas, Lady Bird met and married Lyndon Baines Johnson—a union that changed the course of history for both the state and the nation. Lady Bird used funds from an inheritance to launch her husband's first political campaign, thus initiating a career that would eventually lead both to the White House. She had a keen nose for business, and another of her investments eventually made the Johnsons millionaires.

Soon after that fateful day in 1963 when Lyndon Johnson became the 36th President of the United States, Lady Bird created the First Lady's Committee for a More Beautiful Capital. After the election in 1964, she expanded her vision to include conservation and beautification at the national level, which incorporated a focus on cleaning up the nation's highways. Her efforts produced the Beautification Act of 1965, popularly known as "Lady Bird's Bill," and the Surface Transportation and Uniform Relocation Assistance Act of 1987—funding for the latter requires that highway landscaping projects include planting native flowers, shrubs, and trees and places limits on billboards at these locations. For more than 20 years, Lady Bird personally presented awards to those highway districts in Texas that planted native vegetation to beautify roadsides and adopted mowing schedules that permitted these plants to reseed the rights-of-way. She continued these efforts until her death, and today the native plants that color roadsides, urban parks, and trails across the state and nation mark her enduring legacy.

On her 70th birthday, Lady Bird Johnson founded the National Wildflower Research Center using her funds, 60 acres of land she purchased and donated, and a major financial contribution from her friend, actress Helen Hayes (1900–1993). The facility later moved to a larger site located on 279 acres in the Texas Hill Country (10 miles from downtown Austin) and, on her 85th birthday (1989), was renamed the Lady Bird Johnson Wildflower Center. The Wildflower Center, which is now part of the University of Texas at Austin, supports research and education and serves as a nationwide clearinghouse for information about wildflowers and native plants. Each year, more than 100,000 visitors enjoy the facility's 4.5-acre wildflower garden, the 16-acre arboretum, and a display of some 700 species of native trees. By the Internet, the center's online database fields queries concerning the horticultural and ecological characteristics for more than 7,200 species of plants. The center recently initiated the Millennium Seed Bank Project, which collects seeds from plants native to Texas, some of which helped reestablish dune vegetation destroyed when Hurricane Ike devastated Galveston Island. The center also played a major role in replanting the Lost Pines after a catastrophic fire burned much of this island forest in 2011.

A grove named in Lady Bird's honor was dedicated at Redwood National Park, and among many other recognitions, she posthumously received the Rachel Carson Award from the Audubon Women in Conservation. Her portrait appeared on a postage stamp, and she served on several boards, including those of the National Park Service and National Geographic Society.

Her daughter, Lucy Baines Johnson, provided perhaps the most fitting tribute to her mother's far-reaching impact when she said, "I think there is no legacy she would more treasure than to have helped people recognize the value in preserving and promoting our native land." The Wildflower Center bearing her name and the carpet of native wildflowers gracing roadsides each year testify to Lady Bird's contributions. In her own words, "where flowers bloom, so does hope"—so pause a moment when enjoying a trip through Texas to remember her gift to us all.

Figure 13. This flat stretch of limestone in the Guadalupe River near Hunt (Kerr County) once served as the westbound lane of Farm Road 1340; the eastbound lane ran along the riverbank. Some curbing remains in the riverbed.

and evaporite deposits (e.g., gypsum) mark the locations of ancient shorelines.

Beginning in the Cretaceous Period and continuing into the Miocene Epoch (27–12 mya), the Balcones Fault Zone moved vertically, elevating the Edwards Plateau and Hill Country, while the land to the south and east subsided. Interestingly, the limestone strata were not folded or contorted during the uplift, and the flat-lying layers are visible today in riverbeds, road cuts, and canyon walls throughout the region (fig. 13).

During the millions of years since the region was uplifted, runoff eroded the tableland, creating the familiar topography of the Edwards Plateau. The central plateau is less rugged and broken than the celebrated Hill Country, but erosion unearths rocky slopes and limestone formations in many areas. Between the Devils and Pecos Rivers in the extreme southwestern portion of the Edwards Plateau, the topography shifts to a highly dissected region featuring steep slopes flanking mesa-like highlands.

CLIMATIC CONDITIONS

The Edwards Plateau—especially the Hill Country—experiences both wet years and extended droughts; rainfall amounts usually range between 25 and 35 inches per year, but extremes of 11 inches and 41 inches have been recorded in successive years at the same location. Rainfall patterns are

best described as "erratic" on the eastern margin and "undependable" farther westward. In a relatively normal year, however, rainfall remains low from November through April and peaks in May and June, and a second period of rain usually occurs in September and October. The normal pattern may be interrupted in some years by the remnants of hurricanes that move inland from the Gulf of Mexico. On such occasions, a storm may cause severe flooding, especially when a torrential downpour stalls over an area for several days.

Torrential rainfall and heavy flooding along the Balcones Escarpment may be greater than anywhere else in the world because local conditions—location and physiography—generate conditions that spawn intense storms. The escarpment lies in a transition zone between two climatic regimes—a humid subtropical climate to the south and east, and a semiarid climate to the west. When cold fronts move into the region from the north, unstable air behind these fronts often collides over the escarpment with moisture-laden air arriving from the Gulf of Mexico (fig. 14). The change in elevation along the escarpment forces the moist air mass upward just as it meets the cold, dry air mass, often producing what local meteorologists call "rain bombs"—sudden, intense thunderstorms and flash flooding. Some of the highest rainfall events ever recorded in the world

Figure 14. Intensive thunderstorms build near the eastern edge of the Balcones Escarpment and often produce heavy flooding in the Pedernales River and other rivers in the region. Photograph by Jonathan Gerland.

were generated in this region. As examples, in 1921 a storm near Thrall (Williamson County) produced 36.4 inches of rain in just 18 hours—a world record that still stands—and another near D'Hanis (Medina County) in 1935 dropped 22 inches in less than 3 hours. In combination, the frequency of thunderstorms and physiographic factors favoring rapid runoff make the Balcones Escarpment one of the most flood-prone areas worldwide.

Whereas summer visitors from the Llano Estacado might complain about the region's humidity, residents of Houston or Corpus Christi might find the Hill Country satisfyingly dry. Despite these differences, most would agree that the region is hot—not much of a surprise given that Austin, at the eastern edge of the Edwards Plateau, lies at the same latitude as Cairo, Egypt. The daily high temperature in August averages nearly 97°F, but thermometers in Austin occasionally register 101°F or higher for several days.

Winter temperatures vary considerably from day to day and year to year on the Edwards Plateau. Winter storms—known locally as "cold snaps" or "northers"—sometimes drop temperatures as much as 50°F in a single day. Whimsical cowboys once claimed that northers froze coffee fresh from a campfire so fast that the ice stayed warm for hours. Freezing temperatures and snows, though rare, are somewhat more common in the western areas than in the southern or eastern regions of the plateau. When they occur, such conditions rarely persist for more than a few days—never long enough to freeze the ground. Nevertheless, freezing temperatures occur with enough frequency to keep out tropical and some subtropical vegetation.

BIOPHYSIOGRAPHIC ASSOCIATIONS

Prior to the arrival of Euro-Americans, the Edwards Plateau formed a grassy savanna studded by groves of mesquites, oaks, and junipers (fig. 15). Additionally, the landscape included a mosaic of plant communities maintained by periodic, naturally occurring fires. Records from the early 1800s indicate that grass cover was meager in places, likely because of unpredictable and highly variable rainfall; trees and woody brush were confined chiefly to steep slopes and canyons where fires were less common. Scattered vestiges of these communities remain, but fire suppression, agricultural development, and, at some locations,

Figure 15. The presettlement landscape of the Edwards Plateau may have resembled this oak-grassland savanna, a restored habitat on a well-managed ranch.

extensive urbanization subsequently modified the original vegetation.

Botanists catalog approximately 2,300 species of native vascular plants on the Edwards Plateau. More than 200 additional nonnative species also occupy "wild" habitats (those not directly associated with human influences). Endemic species represent only about 10 percent of the native flora of the Edwards Plateau, but more than 100 of the 400 species endemic to Texas occur only in this region—some are considered endangered because of their limited distribution. For example, Texas Snowbells, small trees producing clusters of small, bell-shaped white flowers in April and May, persist in only a few canyons. The only remaining wild population of another endangered endemic, Texas Wild Rice, grows in a few patches along a limited stretch of the San Marcos River.

Many authorities recognize four biotic associations on the Edwards Plateau, whose respective characteristics provide links with the plateau's major topographic features. Our tour across the region will take us from south to north before veering westward toward the Devils and Pecos Rivers.

BALCONES CANYONLANDS

Where the Balcones Escarpment juts abruptly upward from the South Texas Plains, the plateau features a highly dissected topography embracing numerous springs, streams, and rivers and steep-sided canyons (fig. 16). Although many Texans regard the entire Edwards Plateau as "Hill Country," the margin of the escarpment, more than anywhere else, portrays the enduring vision of purple ridgelines, clear creeks, and, of course, iconic hills.

Within this rumpled expanse, which some ecologists describe as the most distinctive biotic region in Texas, an oak savanna covers the uplands between drainages and extends downward onto exposed midslopes and into some wide alluvial valleys. The assemblage of trees on the highlands includes Plateau Live Oak, Texas Red Oak, Ashe Juniper, Cedar Elm, and Escarpment Black Cherry. Although open areas dominated by native grasses such as Little Bluestem, Indiangrass, and grama grasses were once widespread, fire suppression in recent decades has allowed woodland vegetation to invade the ridgetops. Grasslands remain in heavily grazed areas and pastures where ranchers remove

Figure 16. Steep canyon walls etched into level limestone strata enclose the Frio River and many other rivers in the Hill Country.

Figure 17. A narrow riparian forest lies sheltered by a cliff along the Frio River in Uvalde County (top). Massive Baldcypress trees flank the Guadalupe River and many other rivers and streams flowing through the Edwards Plateau (bottom).

junipers to increase forage production for their livestock.

Where the climate becomes more arid on the western rim of the escarpment, shrubby vegetation replaces oak savanna, but even these species may eventually succumb to prolonged drought. High, flat expanses and south- and west-facing slopes support scattered clumps of Ashe Juniper, oaks, Texas Persimmon, Sotol, Cenizo, and mesquites. The north- and east-facing slopes typically support woodlands dominated by Live Oak.

Many canyons of the Balcones Escarpment orient in a southeasterly direction and are deeply incised enough to provide limited protection from searing heat and sun. Rich in endemic shrubs and small trees such as Texas Persimmon, Texas

Mountain Laurel, Mexican Buckeye, and Agarita, sheltered canyons also afford habitat for many woody species more typical of forests in East Texas. Narrow strips of deciduous trees occur on north-facing slopes just below the limestone caprock (fig. 17). The borders of cool, clear watercourses are often lined with ranks of stately Baldcypress, American Sycamore, and Black Willow—typically eastern species that may have been stranded in Central Texas at the end of the glacial Pleistocene (fig. 17). Similarly, Swamp Rabbits also reach their westernmost limits in the river canyons of the Balcones Escarpment.

Many animals whose life cycles are wholly or partially associated with conditions such as soft soils (fossorial species), the hydrologic effects of faulting (the fauna of aquifers and springs), or specific plant-soil relationships may be limited to either the eastern or western sides of the Balcones Escarpment. For example, Spring Ladies' Tresses, an orchid bearing tall spiral spikes with up to 50 white flowers, inhabits open Blackland Prairie sites lying east of the Balcones Escarpment, whereas regularly moistened limestone outcrops along the escarpment mark the limits of its western congener, Giant Ladies' Tresses. Mexican Ground Squirrels and Prairie Skinks occupy nonrocky, grassland-dominated soils east of the escarpment, whereas Rock Squirrels and Great Plains Skinks occur in the canyons and rocky uplands to the west. All told, about 70 percent of all Texas reptiles and amphibians and high percentages of other vertebrates occurring in Central Texas are limited (either eastward or westward) by the Balcones Escarpment.

EDWARDS PLATEAU WOODLANDS

The elevated, central part of the Edwards Plateau features a gentle terrain of low, flat-topped hills descending into wide, flat valleys. Scattered groves of Plateau Live Oak, Texas Red Oak, and Ashe Juniper once punctuated grassy sites covering the hills and valleys—a savanna maintained by recurring fires started by lightning or Native Americans. Moreover, the fires curtailed the expansion of Ashe Juniper, which remained at low densities on hillsides. Oaks, in contrast, send up viable root sprouts after fires that grow into dense, shrubby thickets known as "oak mottes" and become a common feature of the central plateau. The mottes—then as now—provide a shaded nursery for many shrubs, including Agarita and Texas Persimmon, and provide key nesting habitat for the endangered Black-capped Vireo. The region is renowned for the colorful wildflowers that blanket the landscape after spring rains. The vivid sparkle of Texas Bluebonnets and Golden Waves in pastures and on roadsides dazzles in contrast with the softer hues of Winecups and Texas Paintbrushes.

The deeper upland soils of the Edwards Plateau probably always supported a savanna-like mosaic of grasslands interspersed with woodlands. Intensive

Figure 18. In wet years Ashe Juniper berries provide abundant food for many animals that in turn facilitate seed dispersal.

grazing decreased some prairie grasses, especially Little Bluestem, Indiangrass, and Sideoats Grama. In heavily grazed areas, these once-common species often give way to Curly Mesquite and Purple Threeawn as well as brush species like prickly pears, junipers, Texas Persimmon, and mesquites. Large areas of rangeland are now dominated by an invasive Asian grass, King Ranch Bluestem, which government agencies recommended in the mid-twentieth century for soil stabilization.

Early accounts describe closed-canopy juniper thickets, but these were confined to canyon slopes, especially along the Balcones Escarpment. During the past two centuries, however, two species of juniper—Ashe Juniper throughout the region and Redberry Juniper on the far western plateau—invaded the uplands. "Cedar brakes"—dense stands of juniper—now blanket highlands and slopes in many areas where deeply eroded limestone formations are exposed. The invasion and expansion of cedar brakes are often attributed to periodic droughts, introductions of grazing (and overgrazing) livestock, and elimination of recurring, natural wildfires.

Both junipers are shrubby, multistemmed evergreens rarely exceeding 19 feet in height at maturity. Abundant crops of berries are produced in wet years and provide desirable forage for both mammals and birds (fig. 18). Of these, American Robins may be the most effective agents for

dispersing juniper seeds; perched at overgrazed sites, the birds excrete seeds where reduced competition favors the survival and development of juniper seedlings. In the absence of dispersal agents, the heavy berries simply drop onto the underlying layer of rich soil where they remain protected by decomposing leaves. Upon the death or mechanical removal of the tree, clusters of small seedlings spring up. Few herbaceous plants are capable of germinating or surviving beneath the canopy, but cedar duff is thought to foster germination of Texas Madrone seeds. A showy member of the mint family—Cedar Sage—produces tubular red flowers on spikes arising from a basal rosette of heart-shaped leaves, and it occurs almost exclusively in association with Ashe Juniper.

Juniper trees consume large amounts of groundwater and their dense foliage intercepts rainfall, reducing the amount reaching the ground. Ranchers in the Texas Hill Country generally consider junipers undesirable because they suppress grasses, thereby reducing the carrying capacity for livestock. Consequently, many landowners regularly thin or remove cedar stands to improve both water supplies and livestock forage. The cost of removing juniper is often defrayed by the sale of wood products gathered from cleared lands. Two regional industries harvest

Ashe Junipers for raw materials, but Redberry Junipers lack the dense, oil-bearing heartwood necessary for commercial uses. Straight trunks of mature Ashe Junipers are harvested as "cedar" fence posts (fig. 19). These posts resist decay both above and below the ground. Gnarled Ashe Juniper trunks unsuitable for posts, along with stumps, roots, and branches—often the trimmings from fence-post production—provide small distillation facilities with materials for extracting oils. Aromatic compounds in the oils are blended into soaps, household sprays, and germicidal bathroom cleaners, many of which use the word "pine" in the product name. Obviously, the botanical distinctions between juniper, cedar, and pine, though real, blur into the charm of local cultures.

Years of hunting and trapping as well as agricultural and urban development have reduced or eliminated wildlife once common on the central plateau. Although occasional reports of Black Bears, Mountain Lions, and Red Wolves still surface, all were extirpated from the area long ago. A few Black Bears and Mountain Lions have moved back onto the central plateau, likely after crossing the Rio Grande near Del Rio, but they remain scattered and thinly populated. In contrast, populations of American Badger, Coyote, and White-tailed Deer have increased in recent decades. The increase of

Figure 20. Enchanted Rock, a huge dome of pink Town Mountain Granite, is the largest and most well-known feature of the Llano Uplift. Photograph by Jonathan Gerland.

woodlands has also favored greater numbers of North American Porcupines and expanded the breeding range of White-winged Doves farther northward.

LLANO UPLIFT

Despite the implication of its name, the Llano Uplift is actually a basin. The formation, which covers 1,673 square miles, is sometimes called the Central Mineral Region in recognition of the gold, copper, iron, tourmaline, smoky quartz, Texas blue topaz— the State Stone—and other valuable deposits in the area's Precambrian rocks. Numerous rose-colored domes of mostly barren granitic rocks punctuate the flat to rolling terrain within the depressed area. Visible from afar, Enchanted Rock, with its summit 425 feet above the local ground surface, is the largest of several domes rising prominently above the surrounding plain (fig. 20). It was from this height in 1841 that Texas Ranger Captain Jack Hayes, as part of a survey party out of Fredericksburg,

held off a band of Comanche with his two newly patented Colt revolvers. This well-known landmark and the smaller domes in the area represent the exposed and visible parts of a vast underground granite shield covering more than 62 square miles.

The granite domes appear solid and durable, but in reality they are composed of onion-like layers that continually erode and slough off. Massive sections periodically undergo exfoliation— a process whereby the outer layers break into smaller pieces along lines of parallel sheet fractures and slide downslope, fashioning a domelike structure. As a result, their surfaces present a mosaic of barren granite, jumbled rocks, and shallow soils where grasses, cacti, shrubs, and stunted trees somehow gain a foothold. Cracks and protected areas between boulders often shelter unique communities of small plants such as Spikemoss, Purple Cliffbrake Fern, and Nuttall's Stonecrop. For decades, a lone live oak—now a memory—occupied a prominent spot high on

Enchanted Rock; offspring of the old tree now compete for space among the boulders below.

Climbers struggling to the peak of Enchanted Rock usually pause for breath along the route. While resting, they may notice splotches of color—yellows, oranges, grayish greens, and grays—dotting the rocks (fig. 21). Not paint drops left by a clumsy artist, they are lichens—unique, plantlike organisms that are often the only indication of life on the otherwise barren surfaces. It is tempting, but inaccurate, to call them "plants." Instead, lichens are "composite organisms"—a combination of two, or sometimes three, species of organisms that mutually benefit from a shared structure. The crusty growth combines a photosynthetic organism—either algae or cyanobacteria—with a fungus. The fungus provides its partner with water and minerals mined from the substrate or absorbed from the air and, in return, receives organic food molecules and oxygen from its live-in companion. To further aid the partnership, the fungus also produces colored pigments that shield the delicate chemical processes associated with photosynthesis. Lichens grow slowly and should not be touched—a grayish lichen only 4 inches in diameter may well be over a thousand years old!

After rains, water collects in low spots—weathering pits—where chemical reactions disintegrate the granite and winds remove residual mineral particles when the depressions dry. The pits eventually deepen into vernal pools, which may retain water for several weeks and thereby provide microhabitats in the unforgiving landscape. Water-filled vernal pools often harbor a unique suite of plants and animals. For example, after hatching from unseen eggs, tiny, translucent Fairy Shrimp swim upside down while devouring algae and plankton that spring to life from spores deposited when the pools last held water. Rock Quillwort, an endangered nonflowering plant endemic to vernal pools, also germinates from spores when water fills the depressions. The thin, pale green leaves of this diminutive grasslike plant tower as much as 2 inches above the water's surface (fig. 21). When the pools again dry, the foliage withers and blows away, leaving behind spores to join those of algae and the eggs of Fairy Shrimp as a dustlike layer lining the depression. A process known as cryptobiosis allows

Figure 21. Colorful lichens (top), some more than 1,000 years old, often adorn the granitic surfaces on Enchanted Rock, where vernal pools (bottom) also offer habitat for mats of Rock Quillwort and other diminutive plants. Photographs by Brian R. Chapman and William R. Carr, Lady Bird Johnson Wildflower Center.

these eggs and spores to lie dormant—sometimes for years—in the dry, hot concavities while awaiting the return of moisture conducive to regeneration.

Slopes descending from the plateau surrounding the Llano Uplift support stands of Ashe Juniper and Texas Red Oak, but these species do not occur on the granitic soils within the basin. Blackjack Oak, Catclaw Mimosa, Soaptree Yucca, Honey Mesquite, Little Bluestem, and various dryland grasses cover the land between the domes. Deep, sandy soils within the basin support Basin Bellflower, a species

endemic to the region, and stands of Cedar Elm, Black Hickory, and various oaks. Wild Turkeys and Mourning Doves roost in scattered Post Oaks and Black Hickories at night while Ringtails reconnoiter the rocks below.

For more than 11,000 years, Native American tribes explored the large dome and camped at its base. Many of their legends described eerie creaking and groaning sounds emanating from the rock—likely noises resulting from contraction as the granite cooled after a hot summer day. Early Euro-American settlers named the dome Enchanted Rock based on legends about its supernatural powers. After many decades of private ownership and restricted access, The Nature Conservancy purchased Enchanted Rock and then deeded the property to the State of Texas. Enchanted Rock State Natural Area was opened to visitors in 1984, the same year the site was added to the National Register of Historic Places.

SEMIARID EDWARDS PLATEAU

The western third of the Edwards Plateau represents a transition zone between the arid Trans-Pecos region to the west, wooded savannas to the east, grasslands to the north, and brushlands to the south. Annual precipitation is too low to support the dense cover of woody vegetation found eastward on the plateau.

Although it is hard to imagine today, grasslands once covered much of this area. Beginning in the late nineteenth century, shrublands gradually replaced the shortgrass prairie, resulting in the extirpation of many grassland-dependent species such as Montezuma Quail. The shift to scrubby vegetation—often associated with desertification—began with gradual erosion of the shallow soils resulting from year-round overgrazing by large herds of domestic livestock and control of once-frequent grass fires (fig. 22). The process accelerated during the twentieth century as water tables declined and surface water disappeared for long periods between rains. Today, groves of Ashe and Redberry Juniper, oaks, mesquites, and Papershell Pinyon grow on the rocky mesas and mountains and in the canyons. Curve-billed Thrashers abound in residual patches of grassland dotted with scattered mesquites. Toward the Pecos River, shrubs typical of the Chihuahuan Desert become more abundant, indicating a much drier environment.

Numerous rugged, steep-sided canyons lead to either of the two major tributaries—the Devils and Pecos Rivers, whose rock-strewn channels carry water only after heavy rains. Heat waves bounce from exposed rock surfaces during the day, but deep within shadowy canyon bottoms, small pockets of moisture persist and become havens for Maidenhair Ferns and Red-spotted Toads. Prairie Lizards dart between rocks, peering out as if monitoring their habitat from afar, and Rock Squirrels and White-ankled Mice scramble among the boulders deftly avoiding Black-tailed and Western Diamond-backed Rattlesnakes lurking in the rubble. Black Bears and Mountain Lions occasionally cross the Mexican border to wander unfettered in the canyons. In all, the sun-baked canyons are both scenic and, in their own way, vibrant with life.

Remote and largely unspoiled, the Devils River bisects the semiarid Edwards Plateau for all of its 94-mile length, but only the southern half reliably lives up to the name "river." The river originates where six normally dry tributary canyons converge near Sonora, but the upper part of the river flows only after heavy rains flood one or more of these dusty draws. After flowing underground for stretches of up to 20 miles (fig.23), the water emerges again and flows clear after thorough cleansing by sand, gravel, and limestone during the long subsurface journey. Springs along the lower half of the river gradually increase the volume of permanent flow, and even in the absence of flooding, the current often runs swiftly. Freshwater sponges adhere to submerged rocks and cobble where the river drops over Dolan Falls and splashes through a series of Class IV rapids (infobox 6). Listed as a threatened species, the Devils River Minnow occupies stretches of fast-moving water, but much of this habitat was lost when the Amistad Dam on the Rio Grande inundated the last 12 miles of the Devils River with impounded lake water.

KARST, SINKHOLES, AND CAVES

As raindrops fall, they absorb carbon dioxide in the atmosphere and become mildly acidic before contacting the ground. Consequently, minute layers of soft rocks, such as Edwards Plateau limestone, imperceptibly—but steadily—dissolve each time it rains. Centuries of irregular rainfall slowly sculpt the softer areas of surface limestone, producing a landscape pitted with solution pans, rain pits, and rills (fig. 24). Rainwater also drains

Figure 23. Water in the "Dry Devils River" flows underground for long distances during the dry season (top). With added inflows from several springs along its route, the Devils River flows swiftly for the last half of its course to Amistad Reservoir on the Rio Grande (bottom).

into rock fractures to continue the dissolution process in deeper layers, where it develops karst— a limestone-based topography characterized by sinkholes, caves, and underground drainage systems. On the Edwards Plateau, the development of karst created extensive underground networks that include large aquifers and caves large enough for tour groups to enjoy. The formation of aquifers and caves happened long enough ago in geological time to allow extensive speciation, making the plateau one of the richest areas in the world for karst-endemic invertebrate and fish species.

INFOBOX 6. LIVING SPONGES IN TEXAS RIVERS?

Most people associate sponges with oceans, unaware that a few species also occur in the freshwater systems of Texas, including the Edwards Plateau. Freshwater sponges share many attributes with their marine relatives but rarely grow as large. Easily overlooked or mistaken for algae or "slime" encrusted on underwater rocks, sponges are multicellular organisms lacking either tissues or organs. Instead of such structures, specialized cells fulfill their complex life cycle and basic biological functions.

Water movements influence the growth form of a freshwater sponge—some look like crusts, whereas others of the same species might form spheres or fingerlike projections. Numerous holes of varying sizes perforate the external surfaces of sponges. Water enters through these pores into a large internal cavity and from there continues through a network of incurrent canals to chambers lined with flagella and microvilli. The whiplike action of the flagella pushes the water farther along the canal system, while the microvilli absorb dissolved nutrients and engulf particulate matter in a process known as phagocytosis. The food is then passed along to other cells for digestion. Thus cleared of food, the water is expelled through excurrent canals that lead to a large exit pore.

Freshwater sponges are often bright green because of the extensive populations of algae living within sponge cells. In a symbiotic relationship—mutualism—somewhat similar to that between algae and fungi in lichens, the algae's photosynthetic activities produce oxygen and carbon for the host, whereas the sponge provides nutrients, such as nitrogen and phosphorus, required by the algae. Some sponges remain totally dependent on this relationship and decline in the absence of their mutualistic partner.

The body of a freshwater sponge consists of a mineral skeleton formed by filamentous spicules of silicon bound together by a rigid framework of collagen. Sponges have few predators, likely because the sharp spicules in their tissues function as pincushions that would injure the mouth of any attacker. However, the larvae of insects commonly known as spongeflies parasitize freshwater sponges. The cycle begins when adult spongeflies lay their eggs, protected under a web, on leaves overhanging a river. After hatching, the larvae drop into the water to begin life as ectoparasites on the outer surface of freshwater sponges; using specialized mouthparts, they pierce the cells of their hosts to withdraw nourishment.

After further development, the larvae end their parasitic ways and leave the water in search of cover under rocks or behind tree bark; thus hidden, they spin cocoons and pupate until emerging as adults. Far from being parasites, the omnivorous adults feed on a diverse menu ranging from pollen to animal carcasses.

Individual sponges function as either a male or female during a reproductive season, but gender is not fixed and can vary from year to year. Specialized cells produce either sperm or eggs, depending on the current sex of the individual. Gamete development occurs for only a short period during which a local population reproduces in synchrony. In response to unknown environmental cues, the males in each population simultaneously release their sperm, which drift until they enter the canal systems of female sponges or die. Although the mechanism remains unclear, water circulation in the females likely conveys the sperm to the egg cells for fertilization. Freshwater sponges are viviparous; the larvae are nourished by nurse cells while undergoing extensive development within a female's body. After acquiring a covering of flagella, the larvae are released in a free-swimming form that eventually settle on a suitable substrate and metamorphose into adults.

The flexible nature of sponge cells also permits a form of asexual reproduction known as fragmentation. In this process, small pieces of sponge torn away by currents or other disruptions develop into fully functional sponges if they land on a suitable substrate. Another form of asexual reproduction, however, is much more complex. This occurs when, in response to normal environmental stresses, some freshwater sponges form one or more masses of cells surrounded by a resistant coating. These structures, called gemmules, contain yolk in specialized cells but maintain low metabolic activity and resist adverse conditions, including anoxia. When the stresses wane, the gemmules are released and thereafter absorb their yolk, which increases their metabolic rate and initiates their development into active sponges.

At least ten species of freshwater sponges occur in Texas, but recent discoveries of *Spongilla cenota* in the Llano and Devils Rivers underscore the great diversity of this group in unpolluted waters of the Edwards Plateau, where rock or cobble surfaces at depths of 1.5 to 8 feet provide favorable habitat. In addition to their interesting natural history, sponges also serve as useful bioindicators of healthy freshwater ecosystems.

Figure 24. Rainfall or flooding often forms pits by dissolving softer deposits in exposed limestone surfaces, as shown here near the Pedernales River (Blanco County). Photograph by Jonathan K. Gerland.

SINKHOLES

The sudden collapse of apparently solid ground often makes frightening headlines, especially when a sinkhole occurs in a densely populated urban area. Although sinkholes occasionally develop from human activities, as when a water main breaks or old sewer pipes disintegrate, they occur more commonly in karstic regions. Natural processes create most sinkholes—also known as dolines—when mildly acidic water flows through pores or cracks and into the underlying limestone. As the subsurface limestone dissolves over time, a void enlarges until there is no longer any support for the land above. The sudden collapse forms what is known as a "cover-collapse sinkhole." Solution sinkholes, an alternate form of doline, are also common in the region. These develop where surface water collects in natural depressions and the dissolution of soluble surface layers creates a slope-sided pit that steadily enlarges in width and depth (fig. 25).

Devil's Sinkhole, the largest and most well-known doline on the Edwards Plateau, formed when an underground cavity collapsed and left a void 351 feet deep. Native Americans once camped

Figure 25. The entrance to Longhorn Cavern (Burnet County) provides a fine example of a cover-collapse sinkhole, a solution sinkhole, and solution cave. Photograph by Jonathan K. Gerland.

Figure 26. Mosses line the walls of Devil's Sinkhole. Note the climbing ropes (center) and streaks from falling water droplets. Photograph by Dr. Jean K. Krejca, Zara Environmental, LLC (www.zaraenviromental.com).

around the gaping 40- by 60-foot hole, which appears abruptly on an otherwise flat expanse of sparsely vegetated limestone. The wives of early settlers gave the sinkhole its current name in preference to the less genteel "helluva hole" used by their husbands. The lip of the abyss is undercut, beneath which a circular shaft more than 82 feet in diameter drops nearly straight down before gradually widening into an immense, oval room measuring 250 feet wide by 450 feet long. A central dome composed of fallen rock at the bottom of the pit rises more than 66 feet above the floor (fig. 26). Pools of water extending outward into underground "lakes" on three sides of the room are constantly refreshed from seeps on the shaft's walls. Mosses and lichens color the damp walls wherever light pierces the enveloping gloom.

More than just a geological curiosity, Devil's Sinkhole also pulses with life. In the twilight zone in the upper levels of the pit, Cave Swallows and Eastern Phoebes raise their broods in cup-like nests constructed from mud pellets laboriously attached to rock slabs. Nearby, Honey Bees buzz about pendulous combs dangling beneath an overhanging limestone eave. A dimly lit grotto at the bottom provides seasonal roosting habitat for one to three million Brazilian Free-tailed Bats. Each summer evening, the bats emerge from Devil's Sinkhole and other grottoes in smokelike

columns that quickly dissipate as they disperse in search of moths and other aerial insects. An equally spectacular show awaits in the half light of early morning when the bats return, at first circling several times above the entrance and then swooping headlong down to their roosts below. Thick layers of guano collect on the floor beneath the roosts, providing both habitat and food for a specialized community of invertebrates— guanophiles—adapted to life in a darkened, fetid environment. Two endemic members of this diverse fauna, including a troglobitic isopod, *Cirolanides texensis,* and a troglobitic amphipod, *Stygobromus hadenoecus,* live in the three "lake rooms" at the bottom of the sinkhole, nourished by the abundant organic matter falling into the water. In times past, the thick layer of guano—a rich source of nitrogen—at Devil's Sinkhole was mined for either fertilizer or the production of gunpowder (infobox 7).

Protected within 1,859 acres of state-owned land near Rocksprings (Edwards County), the Devil's Sinkhole State Natural Area is managed by the Texas Parks and Wildlife Department. In partnership with the state agency, a nonprofit organization—the Devil's Sinkhole Society—offers public tours for viewing the wispy "bat tornadoes" at dawn and dusk.

CAVE FORMATIONS

Most of the more than 4,000 known caves in Texas are located in limestone formations on the Edwards Plateau, and many more undoubtedly await discovery. Most limestone caves form in a manner similar to that described for sinkholes, and indeed, many sinkholes collapse into deep caverns, creating new pathways to hidden realms. The Caverns of Sonora, however, formed 1.5 to 5 mya when gases rose upward through a fault zone and mixed with water in an aquifer. The extremely acidic solution dissolved limestone layers, which enlarged the aquifer until the water drained off and left the cavernous space.

As defined by the Texas Speleological Survey, a cave is a naturally occurring cavity with a minimum of 15.5 feet of traverse length and an entrance whose dimensions do not exceed either the length or depth of the cavity. With these criteria, Bexar

INFOBOX 7. GUANO, GUNPOWDER, AND BAT BOMBS

In the warm glow of each tranquil summer evening, thousands of people gather at observation decks near the mouths of sinkholes and caves to thrill at the emergence of smokelike columns. Drifting upward and away into the fading light, the murky wisps are actually thousands of hungry Brazilian Free-tailed Bats departing from subterranean grottoes, popularly known as "bat caves," to feed on flying insects. The spectacle can be observed at several Edwards Plateau caverns and the Devil's Sinkhole, which harbor vast populations of roosting bats during the summer and fall. One large bridge, the Congress Avenue Bridge over Lady Bird Lake in downtown Austin, famously offers a similar evening experience.

Brazilian Free-tailed Bats typically roost within the same zone in a cave year after year and commonly pack themselves densely into clusters of more than 100 bats per square foot. Caves and sinkholes regularly used by large numbers of bats also become known as "guano caves," because guano accumulates beneath bat roosts in deep piles that sometimes extend for great distances. Guano deposits can be quite unsettling, especially when the bats are nervously fluttering above, and visits are usually not permitted and certainly not recommended. Guano, bat urine, and live mites drop from the ceiling in a constant rain. Small gnats fill the fetid air and alight repeatedly on the eyes, nose, and mouth. Ammonia levels in some cave galleries reach levels high enough to bleach hair, but most disconcerting, the guano-covered cave floor appears to be in constant motion—seemingly alive with the undertakings of untold millions of beetles, fleas, mites, ticks, spiders, pseudoscorpions, daddy longlegs, and other troubling creatures. Guano thus serves as both habitat and food source, supporting an incredibly complex community of cave invertebrates that rely on the material as the first link in their food chains. Flatworms, blind crayfish, and other invertebrates are also nourished by guano that falls into permanent pools.

In addition to supporting a unique faunal community, guano caves also played significant roles in historical events. Joseph LeConte (1823–1901), an ardent secessionist

The exodus of Brazilian Free-tailed Bats from roosts beneath Austin's Congress Avenue Bridge draws crowds each summer evening. Photograph contributed by the Austin Convention and Visitors Bureau.

and professor of chemistry and geology at what is now the University of South Carolina, developed for the Confederate Army a method for producing an essential component of gunpowder from guano. After extraction from a cave, guano was dried and mixed with wood ashes before being roasted in a kiln to produce saltpeter, the colloquial name for potassium nitrate. About 2,500 pounds of guano had to be shoveled out of the caves each day to produce just 100 pounds of pure saltpeter crystals. To facilitate removal, mule-drawn rail carts were used to remove the raw material from the deposit in Frio Cave (near Concan). The Confederate Army operated gunpowder kilns at New Braunfels and near Frio Cave to process guano from several caves—the remains of the kilns can still be seen at the Concan location. A simple mixture—seven parts saltpeter mixed with five parts charcoal and five parts sulfur—provided firepower for Confederate guns until the end of the Civil War.

The bats of Frio Cave were again enlisted during the Second World War to support a strange but ambitious effort named Project X-Ray. After watching clouds of bats exiting Carlsbad Caverns in New Mexico, Dr. Lytle S. Adams (1883–1970), a dentist, was driving home on December 7, 1941, when he heard the announcement on his car radio that Pearl Harbor had been attacked. Incensed, he devised a plan for American retaliation. His idea involved tying small, time-fused incendiary bombs to bats, which would be released from airplanes over Japan. He reasoned that the bats would seek shelter in buildings constructed of rice paper and wood on the islands, and when the fuse detonated, the structures would ignite and cause widespread devastation. After the concept received approval by President Franklin D. Roosevelt (1882–1945), traps were placed at Frio Cave and several other area caves to "recruit" the living messengers of destruction. Testing of the "bat bomb" was conducted in December 1943 on a remote area of Dugway Proving Grounds, Utah, where a mock Japanese village had been constructed. When the bats were dropped, they bypassed the target structures, heading instead to newly constructed buildings on a nearby military airfield, which were set ablaze. Although the "bat bomb" test proved effective—albeit misdirected—the project was brought to a halt by a far more effective weapon—the atomic bomb.

County alone has 575 cavities and more than 1,000 caves that occur within 40 miles of San Antonio. At least 137 caves in Texas exceed 990 feet in length, and 132 reach depths of at least 99 feet.

Amazing speleothems—distinctive hanging, upright, or columnar structures—add splendor to some Edwards Plateau caves. The most common speleothems are stalactites, which form when mineralized water solutions drip from cave ceilings. As mildly acidic water percolates through limestone, calcium carbonate in the rock is transformed into a solution of calcium bicarbonate. As each drop falls, a minute ring of calcite remains behind and gradually elongates to form a fragile, hollow tube known as a "soda straw." Growth of these formations depends on many factors, but the average stalactite grows about 0.12 inch per year. Some soda straws become long and delicate, but most often, debris plugs the central tube, causing minerals to accumulate on the outer surface and form a conical structure (fig. 27). When drops fall to the cave floor, the deposits gradually build cones upward, forming stalagmites. Stalactites and stalagmites sometimes meet to form a ceiling-to-floor column, which steadily increases in diameter through the ages. Natural Bridge Caverns, a commercial cave near New Braunfels, features spectacular examples of stalactites and columns.

Calcite speleothems can take several other forms. Flowstones in the form of thin, linear "draperies" develop when mineral-bearing water streams across a sloping surface before dripping downward. Usually translucent, or nearly so, some draperies are called "cave bacon" because brownish, meat-like streaks separate narrow whitish layers. The most delicate speleothems, helictites, defy explanation; they grow outward, not downward or upward, and develop in countless shapes. To imaginative minds, various helictites resemble ribbons, flowers, saws, curly fries, rods, worms, clumps of worms, fishtails, or hands. Perhaps the "butterfly" formation in the Caverns of Sonora (Sutton County) represents the best-known helictite in Texas and remains gorgeous even after part of one wing broke off in 2006. No theory has yet explained what forces shape helictites, but

Figure 27. The droplet about to fall from this soda straw will leave behind a tiny mineral deposit that imperceptibly lengthens the delicate tube (left). Over time, millions of such droplets build stalactites, stalagmites, and columns in karst caves (above).

many believe that wind or capillary action may be involved.

Seven caves in Texas are open to the public. One, Caverns of Sonora, is widely considered the most beautiful cave in the world because of its abundant and distinctive speleothems. All of the "show caves" contain a variety of interesting formations and fossils and allow a glimpse into the mysterious underworld. Nine state-owned "wild caves"—those lacking trails or electric lights—are also open for guided tours.

CAVE FAUNA

At show caves, visitors enjoy an assortment of formations, and most experience a brief period exposed, perhaps for the first time, to a stark environment totally devoid of light. Most tours, however, steer visitors well away from the biological curiosities endemic to caves—the animals adapted to an eccentric life in a dark wilderness.

Descent into a cavern begins in the dimly lit "twilight zone" just inside the entrance. Within this short section, temperature and light regimes vary daily and seasonally even though light penetrating the zone is limited. Ferns, mosses, and a few types of flowering plants—species able to continue photosynthetic activities in reduced light—persist here. Some animals that seek food or shelter in a cavern's threshold venture into the twilight zone but rarely proceed farther.

Beyond the twilight zone, environmental conditions gradually cease to be influenced by season, time of day (or night), or surface weather patterns. The number, size, and orientation of cave entrances may influence airflow, but even so, conditions in the interior remain relatively stable throughout a day or year. Temperature deep within a cave generally mirrors the annual average for the region above.

Few animals venture deep into caves, and fewer still are adapted for survival within a cavern's foreboding recesses. Nevertheless, a specialized branch of biology—biospeleology—is dedicated to the study of cave organisms and their adaptations. Of special interest are those cave-adapted creatures that seemingly "evolved backward." Indeed, fascinating studies await those wishing to discover the genetic mechanisms by which some species lose eyes, pigments, and other structures that remain functional in their aboveground counterparts. To facilitate such research, biospeleologists developed a classification system based on the degree to which these species have adapted to cave existence.

Troglophiles complete their life cycles with equal success both in caves and on the surface. This group includes certain species of insects, spiders, scorpions, crayfish, and salamanders.

Green plants form the base of almost all aboveground food chains, and in their absence cave-dwelling animals necessarily depend on energy from organic matter imported from the outside world. The role of "energy importers" is played by trogloxenes—species that periodically depend on caves for roosting, reproduction, or hibernation but regularly exit, usually to feed. Bats represent the foremost organisms in this group. Bats emerge nightly to feed on moths, beetles, and other insects and return at dawn to congregate in tight clusters on cave walls and ceilings. Beneath these roosts falls a steady rain of fecal droppings and urine, producing deep deposits of nutrient-rich guano on the cave floor (infobox 7).

Other trogloxene species include Cave Crickets and Cave Swallows. Cave Swallows, the only North American birds that require caves for nesting, construct their nests in the twilight zone of caves with large entrances. Unlike bats, these swallows feed during the day and spend nights in their nests or roosting on narrow shelves. Porcupines, skunks, Ringtails, Raccoons, and Bobcats frequently enter caves in Texas, but only Raccoons explore the dark zone. Raccoon droppings provide food for some cave-dwelling invertebrates, but more significantly, the excreta nourish a fungus that serves as an important food for springtails and other organisms.

Troglobites are so adapted to cave conditions that they can no longer cope in the outside world and never venture forth. Typical adaptations include the loss of skin pigmentation and vision (fig. 28). For animals in total darkness, it is no longer beneficial to expend energy to produce pigments for camouflage, protection from the sun, or sexual recognition, and functional eyes are useless. As these species lost their vision, they developed other sensory organs. Eyeless cave fish,

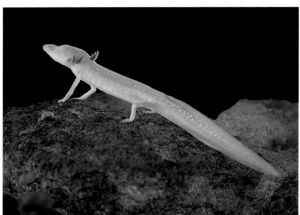

Figure 28. A cave-obligate millipede, *Speodesmus echinourus* (top), in a Travis County cave and the endangered Texas Blind Salamander (bottom), a denizen of the Edwards Aquifer, exhibit the classic features of troglobites—blindness and loss of pigmentation. Photographs by William R. Elliott and Joe N. Fries, US Fish and Wildlife Service.

for example, locate prey and avoid obstacles by detecting minute changes in water pressure with lateral lines or elongated barbels.

The specialized adaptations of troglobites limit their dispersal ability, and consequently many remain confined to either a single cave system or a few caverns within a small area. As a result, many troglobites, such as the Texas Cave Shrimp, are extremely vulnerable to extinction. Species in areas undergoing rapid urbanization are the most at risk. Just a year after the Endangered Species Act of 1966 became law, the Texas Blind Salamander became the first troglobite placed on the endangered species list by the US Fish and Wildlife Service. The salamander, a "poster child" troglobite (fig. 28), faces threats from declining water levels in the aquifer as well as pollution from the city of San Marcos, which lies directly above the aquifer. The species is endemic to the San Marcos Pool of

Figure 29. Barton
Springs, among
others fed by
the Edwards
Aquifer, provides
recreation but
also habitat for
the endangered
Barton Springs
Salamander
(inset).
Photographs
by Paige A.
Najvar and Lisa
O'Donnell (inset).

the Edwards Aquifer, but individuals occasionally
emerge from springs and survive in deep stream
pools.

Although the caves, sinkholes, and aquifers
throughout the Edwards Plateau contain a rich
cave-dwelling fauna, much remains unknown.
Many taxa, especially mites, centipedes, and
miscellaneous insects, remain unidentified and
undescribed, and many cave systems have yet to
be thoroughly explored. Virtually every region
of the Edwards Plateau contains one or more
species endemic only to cave systems in that same
area. Nineteen invertebrates—eight beetles, six
spiders, three harvestmen, an amphipod, and a
pseudoscorpion—are protected by the Endangered
Species Act. Several others are "candidate species"
(the status and vulnerability of their populations
are under review for federal protection). As might
be expected, listing these "cave bugs" generated
public controversy in the Austin and San Antonio
areas, but most of the development projects
temporarily stalled by concerns for these species
were eventually approved after provisions for
protecting the caves they inhabit were guaranteed.

HIGHLIGHTS
LAND OF 1,100 SPRINGS

The Pearl Brewing Company began brewing beer
in 1883 using pure spring water issuing from the
Edwards Aquifer in San Antonio. Just over a century
later, the company developed an advertising
campaign using its most well-known slogan,
"From the country of 1100 springs." Although
the company's estimate of springs in the Texas
Hill Country might not be accurate, the slogan
recognizes the region's many sources of crystal-
clear water bubbling up through limestone layers
perforated like Swiss cheese (fig. 29).

Recognized as one of the most prolific artesian
aquifers in the world, the Edwards Aquifer, located
beneath the southern border of the Edwards
Plateau, discharges about 900,000 acre-feet
of water annually. Water-bearing rock extends
northeast in a 180-mile arc, but the entire aquifer
complex is considerably larger and consists of three
distinct zones: the contributing zone, the recharge
zone, and the artesian zone.

Prior to 1896, most geologists believed that the
underground water in the central part of Texas
originated from the Rocky Mountains. In actuality,

the contributing zone encompasses about 5,400 square miles in the central Hill Country where water collects, often sinking into the ground to be discharged from springs into streams and rivers. Rivers and creeks in the contributing zone flow toward the recharge zone, which runs in a narrow band along the Balcones Escarpment. Outcrops of highly fractured and faulted limestone on the 1,250-square-mile surface of the recharge zone act as a sieve and allow water to trickle into the aquifer. Although some recharge comes from rainwater, approximately 75–80 percent of the water entering the aquifer is supplied by streams and rivers crossing the recharge zone. After heavy rains, some streams on the Edwards Plateau overflow into sinkholes, which transmit the water directly to the aquifer. For example, the large Valdina Farms Sinkhole (Medina County) swallows 1,770 gallons per second during a flood.

Recharge of the Edwards Aquifer is also augmented by contributions from another large water deposit—the Trinity Aquifer—underlying northern portions of the Edwards Aquifer. Where the two water deposits are juxtaposed, upwellings from the Trinity Aquifer add at least 59,000 acre-feet of recharge annually to the Edwards Aquifer. Because of this connection, the aquifers are often referenced as the Edwards-Trinity Aquifer.

Water percolates downward by gravity from the recharge zone through porous limestone to the artesian zone, where the liquid is trapped between impermeable layers. As new water flows into the aquifer, its weight creates tremendous hydraulic pressure on the liquid imprisoned deeper in the formation. The resulting tension forces water upward through faults and wells to burst forth at the surface. When the first municipal well was drilled to supply water for San Antonio, for example, the water gushed upward 26 feet.

Springs gushing from underground aquifers afford a luxuriant microhabitat supporting a distinctive flora and fauna (fig. 30). Colonies of Chatterbox Orchids cling to dripping ledges and thrust their showy orange blossoms above verdant stands of Southern Shield Ferns, Maidenhair Ferns, and horsetails congregated near the water source. A little farther away, dense clumps of Seep Muhly and Little Bluestem protect Western Slimy

Figure 30. Verdant microhabitats often surround the clear, cool springs that erupt from aquifers beneath the Edwards Plateau. Photograph by Paige A. Najvar.

Salamanders and Red-striped Ribbonsnakes from predators.

Although the Pearl Brewing Company no longer exists as a corporate entity and its brewery in San Antonio has closed, the original advertising slogan remains a viable descriptor for the Edwards Plateau. The many springs giving birth to clear rivers flowing through verdant canyons still provide the biological diversity and scenic beauty for which the Texas Hill Country is so justly admired.

HILL COUNTRY RIVERS

Many Texas rivers and their tributaries with headwaters on the plateau owe their origins to springs and, as a result, typically flow year round (fig. 31). The Guadalupe River originates from two spring-fed branches in Kerr County and runs

Figure 31. Clear water from a nearby spring cascades over a small waterfall on Spring Creek (Burnet County), a tributary of the Colorado River. Photograph by Jonathan K. Gerland.

clear and swift beneath high limestone bluffs and ancient Baldcypress trees. Recurring floods along the middle and lower parts of the river prompted construction of a dam several miles upstream from New Braunfels. Completed in 1964, the dam impounded Canyon Lake, a reservoir with approximately 8,230 acres of surface area and 80 miles of shoreline. Although there are no natural lakes in the Texas Hill Country, reservoirs designed for flood control, water storage, and recreation occur on most of the rivers on the Edwards Plateau.

Two rivers, the Colorado and Concho, originate outside the region before crossing the Edwards Plateau. Riffle systems in the Concho and middle Colorado Rivers host the Texas Map Turtle, a species endemic to the Edwards Plateau. Baldcypress, Pecan, American Sycamore, and Black Willow dominate narrow riparian strips, but somewhat larger gallery forests of oaks, elms, hackberries, Black Walnuts, and Eastern Cottonwoods develop on wider floodplains, which occasionally experience catastrophic flooding.

Deep channels and vegetated shallows in several rivers provide habitat for native Guadalupe Bass and introduced Smallmouth Bass; tiny, spectacularly colorful Orangethroat Darters rush from rock to rock in fast-running riffles.

Streamsides are busy places day and night—crevices in canyon walls offer refuge for Texas Alligator Lizards during the day and calling perches for Cliff Chirping Frogs at night. The diminutive frogs call from damp recesses, but their voices are almost drowned by the cacophony from Blanchard's Cricket Frogs and Spotted Chorus Frogs favoring backwater pools left when the rivers change their course. Armadillos shuffle noisily through the floodplain, searching leafy debris for grubs and insects while Painted Buntings, Summer Tanagers, and White-eyed Vireos advertise their territories from perches high in the canopy.

BRIGHT-FACED SONGSTERS

The clear, buzzing songs of Golden-cheeked Warblers—the only bird species nesting exclusively

Figure 32. The endangered Golden-cheeked Warbler (top) requires thin strips of bark exclusively from Ashe Juniper trunks (bottom) for nest construction. Photographs by Steve Maslowski, US Fish and Wildlife Service (top) and Brian R. Chapman (bottom).

in Texas—herald the beginning of spring in the cedar brakes (fig. 32). Upon returning to the Edwards Plateau after overwintering in southern Mexico and Central America, the small, colorful males establish breeding territories typically located in closed-canopy communities near streams or on canyon slopes. After selecting a mate, females construct nests woven from thin strips of bark collected exclusively from mature Ashe Junipers—no other source suffices—but the nests themselves may be located in any suitable tree regardless of species. As a result, the loss of closed-canopy, old-growth stands of Ashe Juniper poses the greatest threat to Golden-cheeked Warblers. Efforts are underway to preserve 76,320 acres of Golden-cheeked Warbler and Black-capped Vireo habitat in both the Balcones Canyonlands National Wildlife Refuge (in Burnet, Travis, and Williamson Counties) and a private initiative in Travis County, the Balcones Canyonlands Preserve System. Several other federal, state, and private entities manage habitat on the Edwards Plateau for the protection of these two endangered birds.

NATURE'S WATER FILTERS

Perhaps the least obvious inhabitants of the Edwards Plateau are the freshwater mussels living largely unnoticed on the bottoms of ponds, streams, and rivers. Of the more than 50 species in Texas, approximately 21 occur in the Texas Hill Country. As filter feeders, freshwater mussels require a bountiful supply of diatoms, desmids, and algae. Because of their diet, mussels rarely occur in headwater pools and streams on the Edwards Plateau, where the cool, clear water flowing directly from aquifers lacks sufficient food. Some species require moderately to swiftly flowing water, but others tolerate a variety of conditions where oxygen levels are high enough and pollution levels are low enough for their survival. The Concho River was named for its abundance of freshwater mussels, especially the Tampico Pearlymussel. In contrast, stretches of the Medina, Guadalupe, and Llano Rivers flowing north of the Balcones Fault Zone generally lack mussel populations because of scouring that disrupts their beds during severe floods.

Because their soft bodies are enclosed by two

shells—or valves—hinged with ligament-like tissue, freshwater mussels are known as bivalves (as are clams and oysters). Adult freshwater mussels spend their lives entirely or partially buried in the bottoms of permanent bodies of water. A muscular "foot" can be extended ventrally from the mantle that encases their inner body, and along with movements of the two valves, it can facilitate both vertical and horizontal travel in the substrate. During warm seasons, mussels reside near the surface of the substrate, where, by slightly opening their valves, they expose two tubelike siphons, which constantly move water containing oxygen and food across the gills and out again. Food particles suspended in the water become entrapped in the gills and then move by ciliary action to the mouth. Mussels can change locations but seldom move as long as the water bears enough essential nutrients for their needs.

Freshwater mussels have a unique but complex reproductive cycle that varies somewhat by species. Typically, males release their sperm, which the females take in through their incurrent siphons. At about the same time, eggs released by females become fertilized on their gills, parts of which serve as brood pouches collectively known as marsupia. Within each marsupium, fertilized eggs develop into tiny parasitic larvae called glochidia; to continue their development, the larvae become parasites that must attach themselves to the gills or skin of a host fish. The glochidia of some species of mussels parasitize only one kind of fish—a classic example of host specificity—whereas others can survive on fishes of several species.

Remarkably, freshwater mussels employ wily ruses to entice fish close enough to transfer their larvae. For example, the Texas Fatmucket—a mussel endemic to the Guadalupe–San Antonio and Colorado drainages of the Edwards Plateau—accomplishes this task with a mantle modified to resemble a minnow complete with eyespot, tail, and waving fins (fig. 33). When a passing fish attempts to dine on the "minnow" protruding seductively from the substrate, the mussel suddenly engulfs the unsuspecting predator with a blast of glochidia. Other mussels acquire hosts by releasing glochidia in gelatinous packets that resemble small minnows or tiny insect larvae. After attaching to a host with

Figure 33. The mantle of the female Broken-rays Mussel resembles a minnow that lures predatory fish near enough to be infected with the mussel's parasitic larvae. Photograph by M. Chris Barnhart.

minute hooks, glochidia embed themselves in the fish's tissues, where they change little in size but develop most of their adult characteristics, all without much harm to the host. When development is complete, a miniature version of an adult mussel breaks free of the host and falls to the bottom. Once there, the now independent mussel becomes a lifelong filter, quietly helping maintain the sparkling waters of the Hill Country.

LOST MAPLES

Relics of the past—fragments of rock fences, sagging farmsteads, and rusted hulks of farm tractors overgrown by the very vegetation they once subjugated—lie scattered across the Edwards Plateau. Less obvious, however, are the biological remnants of bygone ages in which the environment differed significantly from conditions today. Some biological relicts may be the few remaining descendants of a once-large assemblage of related species (taxonomic relicts), or the enduring individuals of a more widespread population (biogeographic relicts).

High canyon walls bordering the headwaters of the upper Sabinal River and adjacent drainages in northwestern Bandera County provide a sheltered enclave for a relict population of Bigtooth Maples (fig. 34). Far removed from any other maple forest today, these isolated trees descended from maples that were once widespread in Texas about 10,000 years ago. Although Texas remained ice-free

Figure 34. Lost Maples, a relict population of Bigtooth Maples, lies sheltered by high canyon walls along the upper Sabinal River.

northward as conditions gradually became too warm and dry for continued survival in the south. A few isolated populations of Bigtooth Maples, however, persisted in protected southern environments such as the Sabinal River Canyon, enabled by the deep, rich soil, dependable water, and shelter from drying wind and searing sun afforded by the dissected canyons of Bandera County.

Lost Maples State Natural Area, near Vanderpool, protects 2,900 acres surrounding the canyons that host the relict population of Bigtooth Maples and rare endemic wildflowers, including Canyon Mock Orange, Big Red Sage, and three recently described new species. In autumn, the leaves transform from green to golden yellow and then turn red before falling—visitors to Lost Maples experience a colorful palette worthy of a calendar and one of the most vivid displays of fall foliage in Texas. Rewarding scenery and a variety of birds await visitors at other seasons, as well. During the spring and summer, for example, energetic trills of Canyon Wrens echo off the sheer limestone walls, and Ruby-throated Hummingbirds clash in aerial combat near Mexican Flame bushes. Above the stream, jewel-like Green Kingfishers flash perch to perch in search of vulnerable prey. The network of sun-dappled canyons at Lost Maples, in addition to ecological importance as a natural refuge for thousands of years, also offers stunning scenery that some describe as the "Yosemite of Texas."

A WORLD WITH OXYGEN

Deep in the heart of Texas—Mason County, to be precise—limestone cliffs along the Llano River date to a time when life consisted predominantly of single-celled organisms so delicate as to barely persist as fossils. These included cyanobacteria—once called blue-green algae—of the late Precambrian Era, a block of time beginning with the Earth's formation 4.6 billion years ago and lasting until about 541 million years ago (about 88 percent of geological history). Cyanobacteria survived in an atmosphere of methane, carbon oxides, and other gases, but it contained essentially no oxygen. Toward the end of the Precambrian, some multicelled, soft-bodied forms shared this environment with the cyanobacteria, but life

during the Pleistocene Epoch, the frosty conditions imposed by northern glaciers nevertheless pushed many species of plants and animals southward. The ancestors of Sugar Maples thus migrated to the cool, wet periglacial environments that developed in the southern half of North America, where, separated geographically, they evolved into eastern and western forms.

With the retreat of the glaciers and a warming climate, the two new forms—the Sugar Maple in the east and Bigtooth Maple in the west—moved

Figure 35. A kayak piloted by Tonya Huston floating near a limestone boulder in the Llano River demonstrates the size of some fossilized stromatolite columns. Photograph by Tony Plutino.

nonetheless remained sparse and uncomplicated for many millions of years.

The Llano's limestone rocks, some of which fell into the riverbed (fig. 35), bear fossils known as stromatolites, laminated structures of fossilized cyanobacteria that evolved more than three billion years ago. When living, they grew as stumpy columns in shallow lagoons of ancient seas. The sticky cap of living cyanobacteria at the top of the columns captured fine sediments with each tidal cycle, thus adding a tissue-thin mineral layer on which developed yet another colony of cyanobacteria—a process that added about 2 inches of height per century.

As time passed, the stromatolites, supplemented by mats of cyanobacteria, nonetheless slowly— very slowly—began changing the physical world. Cyanobacteria lack nuclei, but they are endowed with a marvel of nature's engineering— chloroplasts—and thereby produce photosynthetic oxygen in the same way as do modern green plants. For millions of years, however, dissolved iron in the seawater chemically captured the oxygen, as shown by layers of oxidized iron, primarily hematite,

forming dark bands in Precambrian sedimentary rocks. This period of "mass rusting" ended when the iron became fully saturated, after which a surplus of oxygen accumulated in what is known as the Great Oxygen Event. The Precambrian thus ended, still with a simple biota, but primed by an oxygenated atmosphere.

About 542 million years ago, at a time when oxygen likely reached current levels, life underwent a burst of speciation known as the Cambrian Explosion. Ironically, the arrival of these new forms of life curtailed the distribution and abundance of stromatolites, which thereafter survived only where extremely high water temperatures or salinities excluded herbivores and competitors. Some still persist, notably those protected at Shark Bay World Heritage Site in Western Australia.

The relatively sudden appearance of such a full range of animals—swimmers, crawlers, and burrowers—puzzled Charles Darwin, as no ancestors for these creatures were apparent on which to establish their evolutionary lineage. What is clear, however, is the role played by cyanobacteria, often in the form of stromatolites, in producing an oxygen-rich atmosphere in a developing world—and those in Mason County were part of the action.

EXOTIC SPECIES: THE WORLD'S WILDLIFE IN TEXAS

Travelers crossing the Edwards Plateau often spot animals native to Africa or other semiarid regions of the world. For most, an unexpected glimpse of a Plains Zebra or a Reticulated Giraffe when rounding a highway curve can be surprising—and quite distracting.

By definition, any plant or animal from a foreign area that is transported either intentionally or accidently to another location represents an exotic species. In Texas, however, the term "exotic" is commonly applied to large, nonindigenous mammals and birds, especially those introduced for sport hunting. In addition to two large flightless birds—Emu and Greater Rhea—as many as 40 species of exotic mammals from Africa, Eurasia, and South America roam some well-known large ranches on the Edwards Plateau.

Nilgai—an Asian antelope introduced on the King Ranch in South Texas in 1930—was the first exotic species released in Texas. For many years thereafter, the Texas Parks and Wildlife Department resisted requests to release more exotics, but the agency eventually developed import regulations and relaxed the restrictions. Some landowners maintain exotic animals simply for their novelty or because breeding the captive animals helps conserve a species endangered in its native land, but income from hunting stands foremost as the reason for managing a herd of exotics.

Leasing private land to hunters began in Texas in the early 1920s as a way ranchers might gain a reliable source of income in a region where an unreliable environment too often governed their economic success. Because exotics were not subject to "closed seasons," nonindigenous game animals provided hunters with other options besides the annual season for White-tailed Deer. Indeed, some ranchers obtained steady income from year-round hunts of exotic game. There are, however, some major concerns about "exotic game ranching," including the introduction and spread of diseases and parasites, competition with native wildlife, range degradation, and the uncontrolled expansion of exotic populations.

Importation of exotic species requires quarantines designed to reduce the threat from foreign diseases and parasites, but "mistakes" nonetheless happen. For example, after fulfilling the quarantine, Black Rhinos released on a Texas ranch still carried Tropical Bont Ticks, which serve as vectors for heartwater disease in Africa. In another case, Axis Deer released on the Edwards Plateau suffered an outbreak of malignant catarrhal fever. Underlying these concerns is the worry that native animals may be more vulnerable to foreign diseases than their exotic hosts because they lack long exposure to these pathogens in their evolutionary history.

When exotic animals are introduced, competition often begins between native and domestic animals for the available resources—food, water, and cover. To illustrate, the preferred foods of White-tailed Deer—green, succulent forbs and browse—also dominate the diets of Axis Deer, Sika Deer, Fallow Deer, and Blackbuck Antelope. However, when forbs or browse become scarce, the exotics easily shift to grasses, whereas White-tailed Deer soon face starvation. Because of their adaptability, Sika Deer and other exotics have been likened to "sheep in deer clothing." Given that only so much natural food exists per unit area, exotic ungulates easily outcompete whitetails, especially when both share high-fenced pastures.

Many landowners on the Edwards Plateau and elsewhere in Texas protect their investments in native and exotic wildlife with high (average height 8 feet) "game fences." The fences are intended to control the movements of managed wildlife, reduce immigration of other animals, and deter poaching. Game fences sometimes cause serious biological and ecological issues—vegetation degraded by overbrowsing, for example—but with proper care they often work well if the confined populations remain slightly below carrying capacity. Still, even well-constructed fences cannot prevent escapes, and consequently, Axis Deer and other exotics now range freely on the Edwards Plateau. Among other issues, the growing number of vehicular collisions with Axis Deer raises new legal questions about liability.

More than 70 exotic species now reside in Texas, and most of these are held on the Edwards Plateau. Whereas bluebonnets form an indelible element of the regional landscape, so today do exotic animals. For better or worse, a springtime trip through the Hill Country now features sightings of Emus or Blackbuck Antelope as well as wildflowers.

CONSERVATION AND MANAGEMENT

The ready availability of water from abundant seeps, springs, and rivers on the Edwards Plateau surely influenced the region's long history of human presence. Caves in the region, for example, bear evidence of occupation at least 10,000 years ago, and a prominent hypothesis suggests that overhunting by Paleo-Indians caused the extinction of mammoths and other large mammals of the Ice Age. However, the most lasting environmental impacts coincided with the arrival of settlers. At first, the goats, sheep, and cattle introduced by Spanish settlers simply provided subsistence, and the small herds posed little threat to the character of the vegetation. By the late 1850s, however, ranches with overstocked ranges began depleting much of the original grassland vegetation; palatable species such as Big Bluestem all but vanished under intensive grazing pressure. Shortgrasses, among them Buffalograss, Curly Mesquite, and threeawn grasses, as well as King Ranch Bluestem, replaced the tallgrass. So great was the damage that some evidence suggests that the original grassland composition would not return even if grazing miraculously ended.

Invasive species continue to enter the region from every direction, but the harmful effects, if any, of many of these remain unknown. Red Imported Fire Ants, however, have reduced populations of Eastern Cottontails and both White-footed and Northern Pygmy Mice throughout the Edwards Plateau. These troublesome ants have also invaded hundreds of caves in the region, where they pose a major threat to cave fauna, including many species already listed as endangered or under consideration for listing. Unfortunately, Red Imported Fire Ants are difficult to control, but some toxic baits have at least temporarily eliminated individual colonies.

The region's major environmental threat—urbanization—has accelerated in recent years. Rapid expansions of the human population, subdivisions, and 1- to 10-acre "ranchettes" together degrade native vegetation and threaten the integrity of both surface and underground water systems. Land developed for residential and light industrial uses, especially near the larger cities, invariably changes the dynamics of recharge zones for watersheds and aquifers, as well as lessens water quality itself, commonly because of contaminated runoff from paved surfaces. Increasing demands for water by metropolitan, agricultural, and industrial entities have already reduced the flow of Comal Spring, San Marcos Spring, and many other springs. The survival of many aquatic organisms, including species federally listed as endangered, depends on the continued health of the beleaguered Edwards Aquifer (infobox 8).

Freshwater mussels quickly succumb to pollution and thus serve as sensitive indicators of water quality. To be useful in this regard, however, regular monitoring of their populations and distributions is required, already a necessity for the False Spike, a critically endangered species found only in a short stretch of the Guadalupe River, and five Edwards Plateau species considered candidates for listing as threatened or endangered. Dams or other structures that alter stream flow also threaten freshwater mussels, first because increased siltation upstream suffocates their beds, and second because the diminished flow reduces fertilization in some species or eliminates the habitat requirements of fishes serving as hosts for larvae in others. Obviously, these threats can be identified only if thorough population surveys are conducted before new impoundments interrupt the natural flow of streams and rivers.

According to some authorities, the cascading loss of biotic and genetic diversity in the Edwards Plateau region can be checked only by establishing several large biological reserves, each selected on the basis of its resemblance to pristine conditions. Efforts continue to preserve large tracts of undisturbed habitat within the Balcones Canyonlands National Wildlife Refuge and the Balcones Canyonlands Preserve System. Several other federal, state, and private entities seek sites for managing endangered species. For example,

INFOBOX 8. CLARK HUBBS
Ichthyologist and Eminent Naturalist (1921–2008)

As a boy, Clark Hubbs accompanied his father, Carl—a celebrated ichthyologist and naturalist—on collecting trips, lured in part by rewards of one dollar for discovering a new species and five dollars for a new genus—good money for a lad in the 1930s. Thus began a career of field biology highlighted by a robust work ethic and a love of discovery that would remain a lifelong trademark. Indeed, Clark—at 87—was busy collecting fish and field data just a few weeks before his death.

After receiving a BS in zoology from the University of Michigan in 1942, Hubbs served in the US Army during World War II in the Pacific Theater, notably at Okinawa. When the war ended, he enrolled in Stanford University, where he earned a PhD in 1951; during this period, he was associated with both the Hopkins Marine Station and the Scripps Institution of Oceanography. Before completing his doctorate, Hubbs joined the faculty at the University of Texas at Austin in 1949 as an instructor—the humble beginning of an academic career that lasted for nearly 60 years and produced more than 300 publications. He went on to serve the university in many capacities, including as chair of the Division of Biological Sciences. His distinguished service led to an appointment named in his honor—the Clark Hubbs Regents Professor—which, following his retirement in 1991, continued as the Clark Hubbs Regents Professor Emeritus.

Hubbs sampled more rivers, streams, and springs and collected more fish specimens in Texas than anyone else, but special interests always centered on the spring-fed streams of the Trans-Pecos and Edwards Plateau. Whereas his collections contributed significantly to the conservation of the state's fish fauna, he also acted firsthand in furthering the protection of fishes. He testified as an expert witness in a lawsuit that established the Edwards Aquifer Authority, a state agency whose mission in part ensured that enough spring water remained available for the survival of the San Marcos Gambusia and Fountain Darter. When Hubbs realized that dredging had destroyed the original habitat for the endangered Comanche Springs Pupfish and Pecos Gambusia, which thereafter persisted only in a highly altered canal at Balmorhea State Park, he enlisted the aid of Texas Parks and Wildlife, volunteers, and students from several universities. Their efforts eventually succeeded in diverting water from the canal to re-create the natural habitat for the fish—a desert ciénaga.

Hubbs developed the first taxonomic key for identifying the state's freshwater fish, which may have triggered his last major contribution to the natural history of Texas—a checklist for the fishes of Texas. This project in turn evolved into the Fishes of Texas Online, aided by two of his former students who provided additional information and technical expertise. The mass of data provides the sampling site for every preserved fish ever collected in Texas, including tens of thousands of those contributed by Hubbs himself, plus the taxonomy, characteristics, habitat, and biology for each species. Fishes of Texas Online serves as an invaluable resource for research and conservation of the state's fish fauna as well as a monument to Hubbs and his contributions to ichthyology.

During his career, Hubbs actively participated in several professional organizations. His colleagues elected him president of the American Society of Ichthyologists and Herpetologists, the American Institute of Fishery Research Biologists, the Texas Organization for Endangered Species, and the Texas Academy of Science. He edited *Copeia* and the *Transactions of the American Fisheries Society* and helped found the Southwestern Association of Naturalists, for which he served as editor of its journal, as president, and as a long-term member of the Board of Governors. The association honored him with the W. Frank Blair Eminent Naturalist Award in 1991 and with the George Miksch Sutton Award in Conservation Research in 1997. Still, his greatest and most enduring legacies remain in the students he inspired, the survival of endangered species he championed in his research and conservation efforts, and the threatened aquatic habitats he identified and helped protect. By any reckoning, Clark Hubbs will long be linked with ichthyology in Texas.

in 1985 Travis County purchased and protected 232 acres surrounding Hamilton Pool, a large swimming hole in a grotto formed by a collapsed sinkhole. In addition to the uplands, where stands of mature Ashe Juniper provide nesting material for Golden-cheeked Warblers, the shaded recess near the waterfall tumbling into Hamilton Pool harbors Chatterbox Orchids, Red Bay, Maidenhair Ferns, and a variety of mosses, as well as a nesting site for Cliff Swallows.

INFOBOX 9. THE NATURE OF ROY BEDICHEK (1878–1959)

Adventures with a Texas Naturalist thrust Roy Bedichek into the hearts and minds of readers with a love of nature. Bedichek crafted the book, published in 1947 when he was 69, from three decades of notes accumulated as he wandered across Texas visiting sites from prairie to forest. Usually traveling alone, he often camped out, cooking over an open fire. Then, at the urging of two influential friends, famed historian Walter Prescott Webb and literary giant J. Frank Dobie, Bedichek secluded himself to write about his experiences and observations. For want of an isolated pond and rustic cabin, he instead lived and wrote Walden-like for a year in a large room in a stone building on Webb's ranch near Austin. There, with the companionship of a curious Canyon Wren that popped in and out of a hole in the ceiling, Bedichek wrote at an oak table once in the service of gamblers and confiscated by Texas Rangers. He stocked this hideaway with 1,200 reference books, cooked with iron pots in the fireplace, and for inspiration, gazed across the landscape of the Texas Hill Country.

By any measure, Bedichek had sampled life. He had picked berries in New Jersey, waited tables in Montreal, homesteaded in Oklahoma, slaughtered hogs in Chicago, and labored on river boats on the Ohio. He had also tried his hand with the newspaper business in Fort Worth and San Antonio, taught high school English in San Angelo, and, with a friend, hiked across Europe. This done, Bedichek pedaled a bicycle from Falls County in north-central Texas to Deming, New Mexico, where he edited a local newspaper, served as secretary for the chamber of commerce, owned a small ranch—and married. He had traveled much—and often—since his birth in Illinois and move to Texas with his family six years later. In 1903, Bedichek graduated from the University of Texas, where, in 1925, he would also earn a master's degree.

His job hopping over, Bedichek started work in 1917 with the Austin-based University Interscholastic League, then a part of the University of Texas Bureau of Extension, where he remained until retiring in 1948. His duties required frequent travel, which further enabled his visits to natural areas across the state. On one such trip, he camped among the dunes near Monahans, where he presaged their preservation as a state park—an event realized in 1957. Marveling at the acorn production from the miniature forests of Shinnery Oak among the dunes, he ventured that the fruit-to-wood ratio might be like no other in the world, which remains unproved but is likely accurate. In the Hill Country, he likened the areas cleared of "cedar" to a landscape diseased by leprous spots, where future studies will reveal the effects of this practice on wildlife, perhaps beneficial in some cases, but certainly harmful for Golden-cheeked Warblers.

Fences, Golden Eagles, and especially Northern Mockingbirds held a special place in Bedichek's world. Fences interfere with the healthy circulation of natural life in ways not unlike hardened arteries in the human circulatory system. Still, fences along rights-of-way maintain roadside corridors where native vegetation can persist free from ruinous grazing. Eagles, shot from aircraft for their love of lambs, deserve better, and Bedichek opined that improved range conditions might restore natural prey to levels where the birds would no longer hunt livestock. As for mockingbirds, Bedichek admired their character and mannerisms even more than their song and espoused at length the heresy that they did not at all mock other birds.

Readers can quickly see that *Adventures* is no mere account of nature's splendor, as the book reflects Bedichek's bent for blending scientific objectivity with poetry and philosophy. The text cites top-ranked scientists of the day along with references to the likes of Browning and Whitman—all testimony to his perception of the fullness of the natural world in which we dwell. Not least among these is Tennyson's celebrated "Nature red in tooth and claw," which Bedichek notes is but a partial view of a whole to be seen not as a still, but as a motion picture of the limitless drama of nature. He deplores how technology and mechanization "have broken the rhythm of life," including the redistribution of our population into "huge clots, called cities," and advances Huxley's *Brave New World* as a case in point. Bedichek thus laments, "We have been expelled from an environment in which we were part and parcel in the other life about us," reminding us that "Though inland far we be, Our souls have sight of that immortal sea, Which brought us hither."

At Barton Springs in Austin, a sculpture identifies Philosopher's Rock, named for the site where three titans in the intellectual history of Texas regularly conversed, and one of the bronze likenesses portrays a genteel naturalist sometimes heralded as the state's "Most Civilized Soul."

APPENDIX SCIENTIFIC NAMES

Scientific names of organisms mentioned in the text appear in this appendix. Alternate common names, and scientific names no longer in use but occurring in older sources, are also included in brackets; some accounts include informative notations. Extinct species are noted by an asterisk (*) following the scientific name. Introduced (i.e., exotic) species are noted by a superscript E ([E]) following the scientific name.

BACTERIA, ALGAE, FUNGI, AND LICHENS

Algae, photosynthetic unicellular or multicellular organisms lacking distinct cell and tissue types such as xylem or phloem [singular: alga]

Cyanobacterium, phylum Cyanobacteria [photosynthetic bacteria; plural: Cyanobacteria]

Desmid, unicellular green algae with symmetrical shapes

Diatom, algae possessing cell walls composed of silicon

Fungi, kingdom Fungi [organisms that acquire materials needed for life by dissolving molecules, usually from decaying organisms; singular: fungus]

Lichen, many species [composite organisms—part algae or cyanobacteria, part fungi]

GREEN PLANTS

Agarita, *Mahonia trifoliata*

American Sycamore, *Platanus americanus*

Ashe Juniper, *Juniperus ashei*

Baldcypress, *Taxodium distichum* [Bald Cypress, Bald-Cypress]

Basin Bellflower, *Campanula reverchonii*

Big Bluestem, *Andropogon gerardii*

Big Red Sage, *Salvia pentstemonoides*

Bigtooth Maple, *Acer grandidentatum*

Black Hickory, *Carya texana* [Texas Hickory]

Blackjack Oak, *Quercus marilandica*

Black Walnut, *Juglans nigra*

Black Willow, *Salix nigra*

Bluebonnet, *Lupinus* spp.

Buffalograss, *Buchloe dactyloides*

Bush Muhly, *Muhlenbergia porteri*

Canyon Mock Orange, *Philadelphus ernestii*

Catclaw Mimosa, *Mimosa aculeaticarpa* [Wait-a-Bit, because its recurved thorns catch and hold]

Cedar Elm, *Ulmus crassifolia*

Cedar Sage, *Salvia roemeriana*

Cenizo, *Leucophyllum frutescens* [Texas Purple Sage, Texas Silverleaf, Texas Sage]

Chatterbox Orchid, *Epipactis gigantea*

Coreopsis, *Coreopsis* spp. [several species of brilliant, multiflowered yellow daisies]

Cornflower, *Centaurea cyanus*

Cottonwood, *Populus* spp., see Eastern Cottonwood

Curly Mesquite, *Hilaria belangeri* [Curlymesquite]

Eastern Cottonwood, *Populus deltoides*

Eastern Redcedar, *Juniperus virginiana*

Elm, *Ulmus* spp.

Escarpment Black Cherry, *Prunus serotina* var. *exima*

Firewheel, *Gaillardia pulchella* [Indian Blanket]

Fragrant Ladies' Tresses, *Spiranthes odorata* [Swamp Tresses]

Giant Ladies' Tresses, *Spiranthes praecox*

Golden Wave, *Coreopsis basalis*

Grama grass, *Bouteloua* spp.

Hickory, *Carya* spp.

Honey Mesquite, *Prosopis glandulosa*

Horsetail, *Equisetum* spp.

Indian Blanket, *Gaillardia aestivalis*

Indiangrass, *Sorghastrum nutans* [Yellow Indiangrass]

Juniper, *Juniperus* spp.

King Ranch Bluestem, *Bothriochloa ischaemum* var. *songarica* E

Little Bluestem, *Schizachyrium scoparium* var. *scoparium* [*Andropogon scoparium*]

Live Oak, see Plateau Live Oak

Maidenhair Fern, *Adiantum capillus-veneris*

Mesquite, *Prosopis* spp.

Mexican Buckeye, *Ungnadia speciosa* [Texas Buckeye, Canyon Buckeye]

Mexican Flame, *Anisacanthus quadrifidis* var. *wrightii* [Hummingbird Bush, Wright's Desert Honeysuckle, Flame Acanthus]

Nuttall's Stonecrop, *Sedum nuttallianum*

Oak, *Quercus* spp.

Papershell Pinyon, *Pinus remota*

Pecan, *Carya illinoinensis*

Plateau Live Oak, *Quercus fusiformis* [*Q. fusiformis* var. *virginiana* is Texas Live Oak]

Post Oak, *Quercus stellata*

Prickly pear, *Opuntia* spp.

Purple Cliffbrake Fern, *Pelaea atropurpurea*

Red Bay, *Persea borbonia* [Sweet Bay, Laurel Tree]

Redberry Juniper, *Juniperus pinchotii*

Rock Quillwort, *Isoetes lithophila*

Seep Muhly, *Muhlenbergia reverchonii*

Shinnery Oak, *Quercus havardii* [Havard Oak, Shin Oak, Sand Shinnery Oak]

Sideoats Grama, *Bouteloua curtipendula* [two varieties occur in Texas: var. *curtipendula* with long rhizomes, and var. *caespitosa* lacking rhizomes]

Soaptree Yucca, *Yucca elata*

Sotol, *Dasylirion texanum* [Texas Sotol, Green Sotol]

Spiderwort, *Tradescantia* spp.

Spikemoss, *Selaginella apoda*

Spikerush, *Eleocharis* spp.

Spotted Coralroot, *Corallorhiza maculata*

Spring Ladies' Tresses, *Spiranthes vernalis*

Sugar Maple, *Acer saccharum*

Texas Bluebonnet, *Lupinus texensis*

Texas Madrone, *Arbutus xalapensis*

Texas Mountain Laurel, *Sophora secundiflora*

Texas Paintbrush, *Castilleja indivisa* [Indian Paintbrush]

Texas Persimmon, *Diospyros texana*

Texas Red Oak, *Quercus buckleyi* [Texas Oak]

Texas Snowbells, *Styrax platanifolia texanus*

Texas Wild Rice, *Zizania texana*

Threeawn grass, *Aristida* spp.

Tickseed, *Coreopsis* spp.

Willow, *Salix* spp.

Winecup, *Callirhoe digitata*

INVERTEBRATE ANIMALS

Amphipods, order Amphipoda [small swimming crustaceans]

Broken-rays Mussel, *Lampsilis reeveiana*

Cave crickets, superfamily Rhaphidophoroidea

Crayfish, freshwater crustaceans know as crawdads, crawfish, or mudbugs

Daddy longlegs, order Opiliones [Harvestmen; long-legged spiderlike arachnids]

Fairy shrimp, order Anostraca, order Cladocera, phylum Arthropoda [tiny shrimplike crustaceans]

False Spike, *Quadrula mitchelli*

Harvestmen, see Daddy longlegs

Honey Bee, *Apis mellifera* E [all honey bees in North America were introduced]

Isopods, order Isopoda [crustaceans with seven pairs of legs]

Pseudoscorpion, order Pseudoscorpiones [false scorpions; small arachnids equipped with pincers, but lacking a scorpion-like tail]

Red Imported Fire Ant, *Solenopsis invicta* E [this harmful invasive species should not be confused with native fire ants in the same genus]

Tampico Pearlymussel, *Cyrtonaias tampicoensis*

Texas Cave Shrimp, *Palaemonetes antrorum*

Texas Fatmucket, *Lampsilis bracteata*

Tropical Bont Tick, *Amblyomma variegatum* E

FISHES

Comanche Springs Pupfish, *Cyprinodon elegans*

Devils River Minnow, *Dionda diaboli* [a threatened species]

Fountain Darter, *Etheostoma fonticola* [an endangered species]

Guadalupe Bass, *Micropterus treculii*

Orangethroat Darter, *Etheostoma spectabile*

Pecos Gambusia, *Gambusia nobilis*

San Marcos Gambusia, *Gambusia georgei*

Smallmouth Bass, *Micropterus dolomieu*

AMPHIBIANS

Barton Springs Salamander, *Eurycea sosorum*

Blanchard's Cricket Frog, *Acris blanchardi blanchardi* [*A. crepitans blanchardi*]

Cliff Chirping Frog, *Eleutherodactylus marnockii*

Red-spotted Toad, *Anaxyrus punctatus* [*Bufo punctatus*]

Spotted Chorus Frog, *Pseudacris clarkii*

Strecker's Chorus Frog, *Pseudacris streckeri*

Texas Blind Salamander, *Eurycea rathbuni* [*Typhlomolge rathbuni*]

Western Slimy Salamander, *Plethodon albagula* [*P. glutinosus albagula*]

REPTILES

Black-tailed Rattlesnake, *Crotalus molossus*

Great Plains Skink, *Plestiodon obsoletus* [*Eumeces obsoletus*]

Prairie Lizard, *Sceloparus consobrinus* [*S. undulatus consobrinus*]

Prairie Skink, *Plestiodon septentrionalis* [*Eumeces septentrionalis*]

Red-striped Ribbonsnake, *Thamnophis proximus rubrilineatus*

Texas Alligator Lizard, *Gerrhonotus infernalis*

Texas Tortoise, *Gopherus berlandieri* [Berlandier's Tortoise]

Western Diamond-backed Rattlesnake, *Crotalus atrox*

BIRDS

American Robin, *Turdus migratorius*

Attwater's Prairie-Chicken, *Tympanuchus cupido attwateri* [an endangered subspecies of the Greater Prairie-Chicken]

Black-capped Vireo, *Vireo atricapilla* [*Vireo atricapillus*]

Canyon Wren, *Catherpes mexicanus*

Cave Swallow, *Petrochelidon fulva* [*Hirundo fulva*]

Curve-billed Thrasher, *Toxostoma curvirostre*

Dickcissel, *Spiza americana* [called Black-throated Bunting by Audubon]

Eastern Phoebe, *Sayornis phoebe*

Emu, *Dromaius novaehollandiae* E

Golden-cheeked Warbler, *Setophaga chrysoparia* [*Dendroica chrysoparia*]

Golden Eagle, *Aquila chrysaetos*

Greater Rhea, *Rhea americana* E [American rhea]

Green Kingfisher, *Chloroceryle americana*

Ivory-billed Woodpecker, *Campephilus principalis* * [presumed extinct in North America, but subspecies may persist in Cuba]

Mississippi Kite, *Ictinia mississippiensis*

Montezuma Quail, *Cyrtonyx montezumae*

Mourning Dove, *Zenaida macroura*

Northern Mockingbird, *Mimus polyglottos*

Painted Bunting, *Passerina ciris*

Ruby-throated Hummingbird, *Archilochus colubris*

Summer Tanager, *Piranga rubra*

White-eyed Vireo, *Vireo griseus*

White-winged Dove, *Zenaida asiatica*

Wild Turkey, *Meleagris gallopavo*

MAMMALS

American Badger, *Taxidea taxus*

American Bison, *Bos bison* [incorrectly known as "Buffalo"; *Bison bison*]

Armadillo, see Nine-banded Armadillo

Axis Deer, *Axis axis* E [Chital Deer, Chital]

Bison, see American Bison

Black Bear, *Ursus americanus*

Blackbuck Antelope, *Antilope cervicapra* E

Black Rhinoceros, *Diceros bicornis* E

Bobcat, *Lynx rufus* [*Felis rufus*]

Brazilian Free-tailed Bat, *Tadarida brasiliensis* [Mexican Free-tailed Bat]

Buffalo, see American Bison

Cattle, *Bos taurus*

Cougar, see Mountain Lion

Coyote, *Canis latrans*

Eastern Cottontail, *Sylvilagus floridanus*

Fallow Deer, *Dama dama* E

Mexican Ground Squirrel, *Ictidomys mexicanus* [*Spermophilus mexicanus*]

Mountain Lion, *Puma concolor* [Cougar, Puma, Panther; *Felis concolor*]

Nilgai, *Boselaphus tragocamelus* E

Nine-banded Armadillo, *Dasypus novemcinctus*

North American Porcupine, *Erethizon dorsatum*

Northern Pygmy Mouse, *Baiomys taylori*

Plains Zebra, *Equus quagga* E

Porcupine, see North American Porcupine

Raccoon, *Procyon lotor*

Red Wolf, *Canis rufus* [*C. niger*]

Reticulated Giraffe, *Giraffa camelopardis reticulata* E

Ringtail, *Bassariscus astutus*

Rock Squirrel, *Otospermophilus variegatus* [*Spermophilus variegatus*]

Sika Deer, *Cervus nippon* E

Swamp Rabbit, *Sylvilagus aquaticus*

White-ankled Mouse, *Peromyscus pectoralis*

White-footed Mouse, *Peromyscus leucopus*

White-tailed Deer, *Odocoileus virginianus*

GLOSSARY

Artesian: An adjective used to describe groundwater under positive pressure. An artesian aquifer, when penetrated by a well, may be under enough pressure from overlying rocks to push water upward without the use of mechanical means.

Asexual reproduction: One of several forms of reproduction in which gametes are not exchanged to create new individuals. Examples include sprouts arising from stolons and rhizomes; also budding and cloning.

Bioindicator: A species or community whose presence indicates certain habitat conditions (e.g., soil, salinity, overgrazing).

Carrying capacity: The ability of a habitat to support an animal population without degrading the resources (e.g., overgrazing); often varies from year to year depending on factors such as rainfall. Measured in terms of biomass or animal numbers per unit area.

Coevolution: The adaptations of one species in response to changes in another species. Examples occur when two species have a close, interdependent ecological relationship, such as with predators and prey, or insects and the flowers they pollinate.

Cryptobiosis: A living state in which metabolic activity is temporarily suspended or undetectable.

Desertification: A particular type of land degradation in which an area becomes increasingly arid and assumes the environmental characteristics of a desert.

Doline: A sinkhole; a naturally occurring pit draining underground in karst areas. See **Karst.**

Ectoparasite: A parasite that lives on the exterior of its host. For comparison, see **Endoparasite.**

Edaphic: A descriptive term referring to soils. Texture, chemistry, fertility, and drainage represent edaphic conditions relevant to natural history (e.g., vegetational development and the occurrence of burrowing animals).

Endemic: Term indicating that a species or higher taxon is limited to only a certain region.

Endoparasite: A parasite that lives within an internal body organ or tissue of its host.

Exotic: A species living outside its native distributional range after being introduced there by deliberate or unintentional human activity.

Extinction: Refers to a species no longer existing anywhere. Often misused (e.g., "locally extinct") in situations where "extirpation" is the correct terminology. For comparison, see **Extirpation.**

Extirpation: The absence of a species from part of its former range. For comparison, see **Extinction.**

Food chain: The pathway of food and energy through an ecosystem, typically beginning with plants, followed by herbivores, and ending with predators. Most ecosystems have several food chains that together represent a food web.

Fossorial: A term describing organisms that spend most of their life underground. Examples include earthworms, moles, and pocket gophers.

Guano: The excrement of bats or seabirds.

Guanophile: An animal adapted to living in or on guano deposits.

Helictite: A contorted speleothem found in some limestone caves. Portions of these deposits seem to defy gravity because the axis varies from vertical during stages of growth.

Karst: A landscape formed from limestone, dolomite, or gypsum—soluble rocks deposited by ancient seas—and characterized by cracks or sinkholes leading to underground caves or aquifers.

Microhabitat: A constrained site where the environmental conditions differ enough from those in the surrounding habitat to provide suitable conditions for certain organisms (e.g., the moist soil beneath a decaying log provides a microhabitat for salamanders and certain beetles).

Mutualism: A type of symbiotic relationship in which two species derive benefits from their close association.

Periglacial: Refers to environments affected by glaciers, but not themselves buried under ice (e.g., areas influenced by the cool climate immediately south of the ice sheets once covering much of North America); also, the prevailing conditions (e.g., cool, wet climate).

Phagocytosis: Process by which a cell membrane surrounds a particle on the cell surface and eventually forms a vacuole to take the object into the cell.

Seed bank: The residual source of seeds that persist in the soil until conditions favoring germination return. At a given location, a seed bank may contain several species, each with its own environmental requirements for germination and growth.

Speleothem: A secondary mineral formation typically found in a limestone cave. See **Helictite, Stalactite**, and **Stalagmite.**

Stalactite: A type of rock formation (a speleothem) that hangs from the ceiling of a cave.

Stalagmite: A type of rock formation (a speleothem) that arises from the floor of a cave as the result of mineral-laden water dripping from the cave ceiling.

Succulent: In botany, a plant having thick, fleshy parts adapted to retain water.

Troglobite: An animal obligated to live in a cave because it cannot survive elsewhere. Most troglobitic species lack pigments and functional eyes.

Troglophile: An animal with adaptations allowing it to survive equally well in caves or aboveground.

Trogloxene: An animal that inhabits caves while roosting or hibernating but exits to feed and carry out other activities (e.g., Brazilian Free-tailed Bat).

Viviparous: Giving birth to mobile or nonshelled young.

READINGS AND REFERENCES

The references consulted during the preparation of each chapter, as well as a few suggestions for additional readings of related interest, are presented for each chapter in a format that mirrors the headings and subheadings in the chapter. References consulted for both chapters are listed below and are not repeated elsewhere. Similarly, references used to construct the text for more than one section of a single chapter are listed under the chapter title and are not repeated thereafter. Some references are annotated to provide information about content or significance.

Ammerman, L.K., C.L. Hice, and D.J. Schmidly. 2012. Bats of Texas. Texas A&M University Press, College Station. 305 pp.

Bezanson, D. 2000. Natural vegetation types of Texas and their representation in conservation areas. Unpublished MS thesis, University of Texas, Austin. 215 pp.

Blair, F. 1950. The biotic provinces of Texas. Texas Journal of Science 2:93–117.

Bomar, G.W. 1995. Texas weather. 2nd rev. ed. University of Texas Press, Austin. 287 pp.

Brady, N.C., and R.R. Weil. 2007. The nature and properties of soils. 14th ed. Prentice Hall, Upper Saddle River, NJ. 980 pp.

Carter, W.T. 1931. The soils of Texas. Texas Agricultural Experiment Station Bulletin 431:1–190.

Chapman, B.R., and E.G. Bolen. 2015. Ecology of North America. John Wiley and Sons, Chichester, West Sussex, UK. 334 pp.

———. 2018. The natural history of Texas. Texas A&M University Press, College Station. 373 pp.

Chapman, B.R., and W.I. Lutterschmidt, eds. 2019. Texans

on the brink: Threatened and endangered animals. Texas A&M University Press, College Station. 212 pp.

Correll, D.S., and M.C. Johnston. 1970. The manual of the vascular plants of Texas. Texas Research Foundation, Renner. 1881 pp.

Diggs, G.M., Jr., B.L. Lipscomb, and R.J. O'Kennon. 1999. Shinners & Mahler's illustrated flora of north central Texas. Center for Environmental Studies, Austin College, Sherman, TX, and Botanical Research Institute of Texas, Fort Worth. 1626 pp.

Diggs, G.M., Jr., B.L. Lipscomb, M.D. Reed, and R.J. O'Kennon. 2006. Illustrated flora of East Texas. 3 vols. Botanical Research Institute of Texas, Fort Worth. 1594 pp.

Godfrey, C., G.S. McKee, and H. Oats. 1973. General soils map of Texas. Texas Agricultural Experiment Station Miscellaneous Publication MP-1304.

Gould, F.W. 1969. Texas plants: A checklist and ecological summary. Revised. Texas Agricultural Experiment Station, Texas A&M University, College Station. 112 pp. [Has maps and descriptions of the state's major vegetational areas.]

Graves, J. 2002. Texas rivers. Texas Parks and Wildlife Press, Austin. 144 pp.

Griffith, G., S. Bryce, J. Omernik, and A. Rogers. 2007. Ecoregions of Texas. Texas Commission on Environmental Quality, Austin. 125 pp.

Huser, V. 2000. Rivers of Texas. Texas A&M University Press, College Station. 264 pp.

Larkin, T.J., and G.W. Bomar. 1983. Climatic atlas of Texas. Texas Department of Water Resources LP-192:1–151.

Lockwood, M.W., and B. Freeman. 2014. The TOS handbook of

Texas birds. 2nd ed. Texas A&M University Press, College Station. 403 pp.

Oberholser, H.C. 1974. The bird life of Texas. Edited by E.G. Kincaid Jr. 2 vols. University of Texas Press, Austin. 1069 pp.

Schmidly, D.J. 2002. Texas natural history: A century of change. Texas Tech University Press, Lubbock. 534 pp.

Schmidly, D.J., and R.D. Bradley. 2016. The mammals of Texas. 7th ed. University of Texas Press, Austin. 720 pp.

Sellards, E.H., W.S. Adkins, and F.B. Plummer. 1932. The geology of Texas. University of Texas Bulletin 3232(1):1–1007.

Spearing, D. 1991. Roadside geology of Texas. Mountain Press, Missoula, MT. 418 pp.

Werler, J.E., and J.R. Dixon. 2000. Texas snakes: Identification, distribution, and natural history. University of Texas Press, Austin. 437 pp.

INTRODUCTION
Early Natural History in Texas

Bragg, A.N. 1961. Strecker—Naturalist and man. Bios 32:177–181.

Brown, L., H. Jackson, and J. Brown. 1972. Burrowing behavior of the chorus frog, *Pseudacris streckeri*. Herpetologica 25:325–328.

Burke, H.R. Pioneer Texas naturalists: A contribution to the history of Texas natural history from its beginning to 1940. 111 pp. [An unpublished manuscript provided by the author.]

Casto, S.D. 2001. Texas ornithology during the 1880s. Texas Birds 3(2):14–19.

Evans, H.E. 1997. The natural history of the Long Expedition to the Rocky Mountains, 1819–1920. Oxford University Press, New York. 268 pp.

Flores, D.L., ed. 1984. Jefferson and southwestern exploration: The Freeman and Custis accounts of the Red River Expedition of 1806. University of Oklahoma Press, Norman. 386 pp.

Geiser, S.W. 1948. Naturalists of the frontier. 2nd ed. Southern Methodist University Press, Dallas, TX. 296 pp. [Source for Audubon's quotes.]

Goetzmann, W.H. 1959. Army exploration in the American West, 1803–1863. Yale University Press, New Haven, CT. 509 pp.

———. 1966. Exploration and empire: The explorer and the scientist in winning the American West. Knopf, New York. 656 pp.

Goyle, M.A. 1991. A life among the Texas flora: Ferdinand Lindheimer's letters to George Engelmann. Texas A&M University Press, College Station. 236 pp.

Lawson, R.M. 2012. Frontier naturalist: Jean Louis Berlandier and the exploration of northern Mexico. University of New Mexico Press, Albuquerque. 262 pp.

Peterson, R.T. 1963. A field guide to the birds of Texas and adjacent states. Houghton Mifflin, Boston. 304 pp. [The original edition, cited here, was later revised.]

Romer, A.S. 1927. Notes on the Permo-Carboniferous reptile *Dimetrodon*. Journal of Geology 35:673–689.

Schuler, E.W. 1917. Dinosaur tracks in the Glen Rose limestone near Glen Rose Texas. American Journal of Science 44:294–298.

Establishing Ecological Boundaries

Daubenmire, R.F. 1938. Merriam's life zones of North America. Quarterly Review of Biology 13:327–332.

Dice, L.R. 1943. The biotic provinces of North America. University of Michigan Press, Ann Arbor. 78 pp.

Edwards, R.J., G. Longley, R. Moss, et al. 1989. A classification of Texas aquatic communities with special consideration toward the conservation of endangered and threatened taxa. Texas Journal of Science 41:231–240.

Evans, F.C. 1978. Lee Raymond Dice (1887–1977). Journal of Mammalogy 59:635–644.

Evans, J.A. 1955. Use and misuse of the biotic province concept. American Naturalist 89(844):21–28.

Omernik, J.M. 2004. Perspectives on the nature and definition of ecological regions. Environmental Management 34 (Supplement 1):s27–s38.

Sterling, K.B. 1977. The last of the naturalists: The career of C. Hart Merriam. Arno Press, New York. 472 pp.

Telfair, R.C., II. 2009. Vegetation of Texas: Concept and commentary. Journal of the Botanical Research Institute of Texas 3:395–399.

The State of Natural History

Enderson, J.H., and D.D. Berger. 1970. Pesticides: Eggshell thinness and lowered production of young in prairie falcons. BioScience 20:355–356.

Grant, P.R. 2000. What does it mean to be a naturalist at the end of the twentieth century? American Naturalist 155:1–12.

Pyle, R.M. 2001. The rise and fall of natural history. Orion (Autumn):16–23.

Schmidly, D.J. 2005. What it means to be a naturalist and the future of natural history at American universities. Journal of Mammalogy 86:449–456.

Weigl, P.D. 2009. The natural history conundrum revisited: Mammalogy begins at home. Journal of Mammalogy 90:265–269.

Wheeler, Q.D., P.H. Raven, and E.O. Wilson. 2004. Taxonomy: Impediment or expedient? Science 303:285.

Wilcove, D.S., and T. Eisner. 2000. The impending extinction of natural history. Chronicle of Higher Education 47(3):B24.

Wilson, E.O. 1994. Naturalist. Island Press, Washington, DC. 380 pp.

Infobox 1. Vernon O. Bailey (1864–1942): Field Naturalist of the Old School

Bailey, V. 1905. Biological survey of Texas. Fauna of North America No. 25. US Department of Agriculture, Washington, DC. 222 pp.

———. 1919. A new subspecies of beaver from North Dakota. Journal of Mammalogy 1:31–32.

Kofalk, H. 1989. No woman tenderfoot: Frances Merriam Bailey, pioneer naturalist. Texas A&M University Press, College Station. 225 pp.

Schmidly, D.J. 2019. Vernon Bailey: Writings of a field naturalist on the frontier. Texas A&M University Press, College Station. 452 pp.

Zahniser, H. 1942. Vernon Orlando Bailey, 1864–1942. Science 96:6–7.

Infobox 2. *The Bird Life of Texas*: The Life Work of Harry C. Oberholser (1870–1963)

Aldrich, J.W. 1968. In memoriam: Harry Church Oberholser. Auk 85:25–29.

Casto, S.D. 2001. Oberholser's bibliography of Texas birds. Bulletin of the Texas Ornithological Society 34:24–25.

———. 2014. Harry Church Oberholser and *The Bird Life of Texas*. Bulletin of the Texas Ornithological Society 45:30–44.

Casto, S.D., and H.R. Burke. 2007. Louis Agassiz Fuertes and the biological survey of Trans-Pecos Texas. Bulletin of the Texas Ornithological Society 40:49–61.

Chapman, F.M. 1928. In memoriam: Louis Agassiz Fuertes, 1874–1927. Auk 45:1–26.

Morony, J.J. 1976. The bird life of Texas (review). Auk 93:393-396.

Infobox 3. W. Frank Blair (1912–1985): Herpetologist and Evolutionary Biologist

Blair, W.F. 1960.The rusty lizard: A population study. University of Texas Press, Austin. 185 pp.

———. 1972. Evolution of the genus *Bufo*. University of Texas Press, Austin. 459 pp.

Blair, W.F., A.P. Blair, P. Broadkorb, et al. 1957. Vertebrates of the United States. McGraw-Hill, New York. 819 pp. [A second edition appeared in 1968.]

Dice, L.R. 1943. The biotic provinces of North America. University of Michigan Press, Ann Arbor. 78 pp.

Hubbs, C. 1985. William Franklin Blair. Copeia 1985:529-531.

Leatherwood, A. 2010. Blair, William Franklin. Handbook of Texas online. Texas State Historical Association. http://www.tshaonline.org/handbook/online/articles/fb147 (accessed 25 June 2015).

Infobox 4. Frank W. Gould (1913–1981): Botanist

Gould, F.W. 1968. Grass systematics. McGraw-Hill, New York. 382 pp.

———. 1969. Texas Plants: A checklist and ecological summary. Rev. ed. Texas Agricultural Experiment Station, Texas A&M University, College Station. 112 pp.

Gould, L. 1981. Frank Walton Gould, 1913-1981. Annals of the Missouri Botanical Garden 68:1. [Obituary by Gould's wife, Lucile.]

Hatch, S.L. 1981. Frank Walton Gould. Taxon 30:733.

Edwards Plateau

Enquist, M. 1987. Wildflowers of the Texas Hill Country. Lone Star Botanical, Austin, TX. 275 pp.

Goetze, J.R. 1998. The mammals of the Edwards Plateau, Texas. Special Publications, Museum Texas Tech University 41:1-263.

Graves, J., and W. Meinzer. 2003. Texas Hill Country. University of Texas Press, Austin. 119 pp. [Source of the chapter epigraph.]

Matthews, W.H. 1951. Some aspects of reef paleontology and lithology in the Edwards Formation of Texas. Texas Journal of Science 3:217-226.

Riskind, D.H., and D.D. Diamond. 1988. An introduction to environments and vegetation. Pp. 1-16 *in* Edwards Plateau vegetation: Plant ecological studies in central Texas (B.B. Amos and F.R. Gehlbach, eds.). Baylor University Press, Waco, TX. 144 pp.

Rose, P.R. 1992. Edwards Group, surface and subsurface, Central Texas. University of Texas, Bureau of Economic Geology Report 72:1-198.

Structure and Climate

GEOCHRONOLOGY AND STRUCTURE

Abbott, P.L., Jr., and C.M. Woodruff, eds. 1986. The Balcones Escarpment: Geology, hydrology, ecology, and social development. Geological Society of America, San Antonio, TX. 200 pp.

Frost, J.G. 1967. Edwards limestone of Central Texas. Pp. 133-157 *in* Comanchean (Lower Cretaceous) stratigraphy and paleontology of Texas (L. Hendricks, ed.). Society of Economic Paleontologists and Mineralogists, Permian Basin Section, Midland, TX. 411 pp.

Hardin, R.W. 1987. The Edwards Aquifer: Underground river of Texas. Guadalupe-Blanco River Authority, Sequin, TX. 63 pp.

Lewis, J.G. 2014. North Harris Geology Hill Country field trip. Geology Department, Lone Star College-North Harris, Houston, TX. 33 pp. [Unpublished field trip guide.]

Mosher, S. 2006. Mesoproterozoic tectonic evolution of the southern margin of Laurentia: Llano Uplift. Jackson School of Geosciences, University of Texas, Austin. http://www.geo.utexas.edu/faculty/mosher/llano.htm (accessed 17 June 2015).

Peterson, J.F. 1988. Enchanted Rock State Natural Area: A guidebook to the landforms. Terra Cognita Press, San Antonio, TX. 56 pp.

Rougvie, J.R., W.D. Carlson, P. Copeland, and J.N. Connelly. 1999. Late thermal evolution of Proterozoic rocks in the northeastern Llano Uplift, Central Texas. Precambrian Research 94:49-72.

Toomey, R.S., III, M.D. Blum, and S. Valastro Jr. 1993. Late Quaternary climates and environments of the Edwards Plateau, Texas. Global and Planetary Change 7:299-320.

CLIMATIC CONDITIONS

Bishop, A.L. 1977. Flood potential of the Bosque Basin. Baylor Geological Studies Bulletin 33:1-36.

Caran, S.C., and V.R. Baker. 1986. Flooding along the Balcones Escarpment. Pp. 1-14 *in* The Balcones Escarpment (C.M. Woodruff Jr. and P.L. Abbott, eds.). Geological Society of America Annual Meeting, San Antonio, TX. 198 pp.

National Weather Service. 1979. The disastrous Texas flash floods of August 1-4, 1978. National Disaster Survey Report 79-1. National Oceanic and Atmospheric Administration, Washington, DC. 153 pp.

Slade, R.M., Jr. 1986. Large rainstorms along the Balcones Escarpment in Central Texas. Pp. 15-19 *in* The Balcones Escarpment (C.M.

Woodruff Jr. and P.L. Abbott, eds.). Geological Society of America Annual Meeting, San Antonio, TX. 198 pp.

Biophysiographic Associations

Amos, B.B., and F.R. Gehlbach. 1988. Summary. Pp. 115–119 *in* Edwards Plateau vegetation: Plant ecological studies in Central Texas (B.B. Amos and F.R. Gehlbach, eds.). Baylor University Press, Waco, TX. 144 pp.

McMahan, C.A., R.G. Frye, and K.L. Brown. 1984. The vegetation types of Texas including cropland: An illustrated synopsis to accompany the map. Texas Parks and Wildlife Department, Wildlife Division, Austin. 40 pp.

Weniger, D. 1988. Vegetation before 1860. Pp. 17–24 *in* Edwards Plateau vegetation: Plant ecological studies in Central Texas (B.B. Amos and F.R. Gehlbach, eds.). Baylor University Press, Waco, TX. 144 pp.

BALCONES CANYONLANDS

Baccus, J.T., and M.W. Wallace. 1997. Distribution and habitat affinity of the Swamp Rabbit (*Sylvilagus aquaticus*: Lagomorpha: Leporidae) on the Edwards Plateau of Texas. Occasional Papers, Museum of Texas Tech University 167:1–13.

Emery, H.P. 1977. Current status of Texas Wild Rice (*Zizania texana* Hitchc.). Southwestern Naturalist 22:393–394.

Gonsoulin, G.J. 1974. A revision of *Styrax* (Styracaceae) in North America, Central America, and the Caribbean. Sida 5:191–258.

Neck, R.W. 1986. The Balcones Fault Zone as a major zoogeographic feature. Pp. 35–40 *in* The Balcones Escarpment (C.M. Woodruff Jr. and P.L. Abbott, eds.). Geological Society of America Annual Meeting, San Antonio, TX. 198 pp.

http://www.lib.utexas.edu/geo/balcones_escarpment/page35-40.html (accessed 14 June 2015).

Poole, J., and D.E. Bowles. 1999. Habitat characterization of Texas Wild Rice (*Zizania texana* Hitchcock), an endangered aquatic macrophyte from the San Marcos River, TX, USA. Aquatic Conservation: Marine and Freshwater Ecosystems 9:291–302.

EDWARDS PLATEAU WOODLANDS

Cartwright, W.J. 1966. The cedar choppers. Southwestern Historical Quarterly 70:247–255.

Dye, K.L., D.N. Ueckert, and S.G. Whisenant. 1995. Redberry Juniper-herbaceous understory interactions. Journal of Range Management 48:100–107.

Foster, J.H. 1917. The spread of timbered areas in Central Texas. Journal of Forestry 15:442–445.

Garriga, M., A.P. Thurow, T. Thurow, et al. 2015. Commercial value of juniper on the Edwards Plateau. Texas Natural Resources Server, Texas AgriLife Research and Extension Center, College Station. 11 pp. http://texnat.tamu.edu/library/symposia/juniper-ecology-and-management/ (accessed 15 June 2015).

Gehlbach, F.R. 1988. Forests and woodlands of the northeastern Balcones Escarpment. Pp. 57–77 *in* Edwards Plateau vegetation: Plant ecological studies in Central Texas (B.B. Amos and F.R. Gehlbach, eds.). Baylor University Press, Waco, TX. 144 pp.

Griffin, R.C., and B.A. McCarl. 1989. Brushland management for increased water yield in Texas. Water Resources Bulletin 25:175–186.

Smeins, F.E., and S.D. Fuhlendorf. 2015. Biology and ecology of Ashe Juniper. Texas Natural Resources Server, Texas AgriLife Research

and Extension Center, College Station. 16 pp. http://texnat.tamu.edu/library/symposia/juniper-ecology-and-management/ (accessed 15 June 2015).

Taylor, C.A., ed. 1994. Juniper symposium 1994. Technical Report 94-2. Texas A&M University Research Station, Sonora. 80 pp.

Van Auken, O.W., A.L. Ford, and J.L. Allen. 1981. An ecological comparison of upland deciduous and evergreen forests of Central Texas. American Journal of Botany 68:1249–1256.

Van Auken, O.W., A.L. Ford, A. Stein, and A.G. Stein. 1980. Woody vegetation of the upland plant communities in the southern Edwards Plateau. Texas Journal of Science 32:23–34.

LLANO UPLIFT

Allred, L. 2009. Enchanted Rock: A natural and human history. University of Texas Press, Austin. 314 pp.

Kennedy, I. 2010. The history of Enchanted Rock in the Texas Hill Country. Xlibris, Bloomington, IN. 40 pp.

SEMIARID EDWARDS PLATEAU

Brant, J.G., and R.C. Dowler. 2001. The mammals of Devils River State Natural Area, Texas. Occasional Papers, Museum of Texas Tech University 211:1–32.

Bray, W.L. 1901. The ecological relations of the vegetation of western Texas. Botanical Gazette 32:99–291.

Cottle, H.J. 1931. Studies in the vegetation of southwestern Texas. Ecology 12:105–155.

Dearen, P. 2011. Devils River: Treacherous twin to the Pecos, 1535–1900. Texas Christian University Press, Fort Worth. 224 pp.

Powell, A.M. 1998. Trees and shrubs of the Trans-Pecos and adjacent areas. University of Texas Press, Austin. 498 pp.

Karst, Sinkholes, and Caves

Ford, D.C., and P.D. Williams. 2007. Karst hydrogeology and geomorphology. John Wiley and Sons, Chichester, West Sussex, UK. 576 pp.

Hovorka, S., R. Mace, and E. Collins. 1995. Regional distribution of permeability in the Edwards Aquifer. Gulf Coast Association of Geological Societies Transactions 45:259–265.

Veni, G. 2013. Government Canyon State Natural Area: An emerging model for karst management. Proceedings of the 13th Sinkhole Conference, Natural Cave and Karst Research Institute Symposium 2:433–440.

SINKHOLES

Hunt, B.B, B.A. Smith, M.T. Adams, et al. 2013. Cover-collapse sinkhole development in the Cretaceous Edwards Limestone, Central Texas. Proceedings of the 13th Sinkhole Conference, Natural Cave and Karst Research Institute Symposium 2:89–102.

Parent, L. 2008. Official guide to Texas state parks and historic sites. Rev. ed. University of Texas Press, Austin. 200 pp. [Includes Devil's Sinkhole.]

Reddell, J.R., and A.R. Smith. 1965. The caves of Edwards County. Texas Speleological Survey 2(5–6):19–28.

White, P.J. 1948. The Devil's Sinkhole. Bulletin of the National Speleological Society 10:2–14.

Williams, P. 2004. Dolines. Pp. 305–310 in Encyclopedia of caves and karst science (J. Gunn, ed.). Taylor and Francis, New York. 902 pp.

CAVE FORMATIONS

Elliott, W.R., and G. Veni, eds. 1994. The caves and karst of Texas. 1994 Convention Guidebook. National Speleological Society, Huntsville, AL. 342 pp.

Fieseler, R., J. Jasek, and M. Jasek. 1978. An introduction to the caves of Texas. National Speleological Society Guidebook 19:93–94.

Kastning, E.H., Jr. 1983. Relict caves as evidence of landscape and aquifer evolution in a deeply dissected carbonate terrain: Southwest Edwards Plateau, Texas. Journal of Hydrology 61:89–112.

Palmer, A.N. 2009. Cave geology. Cave Books, Cave Research Foundation, Dayton, OH. 454 pp.

Pittman, B. 1999. Texas caves. Texas A&M University Press, College Station. 122 pp.

Reddell, J.A. 1961. The caves of Uvalde County, part I. Texas Speleological Survey 1(3):1–34.

———. 1963. The caves of Uvalde County, part II. Texas Speleological Survey 1(7):1–53.

CAVE FAUNA

Bechler, D.L. 1986. Pheromonal and tactile communication in the subterranean salamander, *Typhlomolge rathbuni*. Proceedings of the Ninth International Congress of Speleology, Barcelona, Spain 2:120–122.

Betke, M., D.E. Hirsch, N.C. Makris, et al. 2008. Thermal imaging reveals significantly smaller Brazilian Free-tailed Bat colonies than previously estimated. Journal of Mammalogy 89:18–24.

Lundelius, E.L., and B.H. Slaughter. 2014. Natural history of Texas caves. Texas Speleological Survey Special Publication, Austin.

174 pp. [Reprint of the 1971 publication.]

Reddell, J.A. 1994. The cave fauna of Texas with special reference to the western Edwards Plateau. Pp. 31–50 in The caves and karst of Texas (W.R. Elliott and G. Veni, eds.). National Speleological Society, Huntsville, AL. 252 pp.

Sealander, R.K., and J.K. Baker. 1957. The Cave Swallow in Texas. Condor 59:345–363.

Stejneger, L. 1896. Description of a new genus and species of blind tailed batrachians from the subterranean water of Texas. Proceedings of the US National Museum 18:619–621.

Strenth, N.E. 1976. A review of the systematics and zoogeography of the freshwater species of *Palaemonetes* Heller of North America (Crustacea: Decapoda). Smithsonian Contributions in Zoology 228:1–27.

US Fish and Wildlife Service. 2003. Endangered and threatened wildlife and plants: Designation of critical habitat for seven Bexar County, TX, invertebrate species. Federal Register 68:17155–17231.

Highlights

LAND OF 1,100 SPRINGS

Ashworth, J.B., and J. Hopkins. 1995. The aquifers of Texas. Texas Water Quality Development Board Report 345. Austin. 69 pp.

Bousman, C.B., and D. L. Nickels, eds. 2003. Archaeological testing of the Burleson Homestead at 41HY37 Hays County, Texas. Archaeological Studies Report No. 4. Center for Archaeological Studies, Texas State University, San Marcos.

Brune, G. 1981. Springs of Texas. Branch-Smith, Fort Worth, TX. 566 pp.

Edwards, R.J., G.P. Garrett, and N.L. Allan. 2001. Aquifer-dependent fishes of the Edwards Plateau Region. Pp. 253–268 in Aquifers of West Texas (R.E. Mace, W.F. Mullican III, and E.S. Angle, eds.). Texas Water Development Board Report 356. Austin. 263 pp.

Longley, G. 1981. The Edwards Aquifer: Earth's most diverse groundwater ecosystem? International Journal of Speleology 11:123–128.

———. 1986. The biota of the Edwards Aquifer and implications for paleozoogeography. Pp. 51–54 in The Balcones Escarpment: Geology, hydrology, ecology and social development in Central Texas (P.L. Abbott and C.M. Woodruff Jr., eds.). Geological Society of America, Boulder, CO. 198 pp.

McKinney, D.C., and D.W. Watkins Jr. 1993. Management of the Edwards Aquifer: A critical assessment. Technical Report CRWR 244. Center for Research in Water Resources, Bureau of Engineering Research, University of Texas at Austin. 94 pp.

Orchard, C.D., and T.N. Campbell. 1954. Evidence of early men from the vicinity of San Antonio, Texas. Texas Journal of Science 6:454–465.

HILL COUNTRY RIVERS

Gregory, S.V., F.J. Swanson, W.A. McKee, and K.W. Cummins. 1991. An ecosystem perspective of riparian zones. BioScience 41:540–551.

Wagner, M. 2003. Managing riparian habitats for wildlife. Texas Parks and Wildlife Department, Austin. 6 pp.

BRIGHT-FACED SONGSTERS

Kroll, J.C. 1980. Habitat requirements of the Golden-cheeked Warbler: Management implications.

Journal of Range Management 33:60–65.

Pulich, W. 1976. The Golden-cheeked Warbler: A bioecological study. Texas Parks and Wildlife Department, Austin. 172 pp.

Rappole, J.H., D. King, J. Diez, and J.V. Rivera. 2005. Factors affecting population size in Texas' Golden-cheeked Warbler. Endangered Species Update 22:95–103.

US Fish and Wildlife Service. 1992. Golden-cheeked Warbler recovery plan. US Fish and Wildlife Service, Endangered Species Office, Albuquerque, NM. 88 pp.

NATURE'S WATER FILTERS

Howells, R.G. 2013. Field guide to Texas freshwater mussels. Biostudies, Kerrville, TX. 141 pp.

Howells, R.G., R.W. Neck, and H.D. Murray. 1996. Freshwater mussels of Texas. Texas Parks and Wildlife Department, Austin. 218 pp.

Parmalee, P.W., and A.E. Bogan. 1998. The freshwater mussels of Tennessee. University of Tennessee Press, Knoxville. 328 pp.

LOST MAPLES

Habel, J.C., and T. Assmann, eds. 2010. Relict species: Phylogeography and conservation biology. Springer-Verlag, Berlin. 451 pp.

McGee, B.K., and R.W. Manning. 2000. Mammals of Lost Maples State Natural Area, Texas. Occasional Papers, Museum of Texas Tech University 198:1–24.

A WORLD WITH OXYGEN

Canfield, D.E. 2014. Oxygen, a four billion year history. Princeton University Press, Princeton, NJ. 196 pp.

Gould, S.J. 1989. Wonderful life: The Burgess Shale and the nature of history. W.W. Norton, New York. 347 pp.

Leis, B., and B.L. Stinchcomb. 2015.

Stromatolites: Ancient, beautiful, and earth-altering. Schiffer, Atglen, PA. 176 pp.

Lyons, T.W., C.T. Reinhard, and N.J. Planavsky. 2014. The rise of oxygen in Earth's early ocean and atmosphere. Nature 506:307–315.

Mills, D.B., and D.E. Canfield. 2014. Oxygen and animal evolution: Did a rise of atmospheric oxygen "trigger" the origin of animals? Bioessays 36:1145–1155.

Plutino, T. 2009. Mason's world class stromatolites and thrombolites. Mason County News 134(9):B10, March 4.

EXOTIC SPECIES: THE WORLD'S WILDLIFE IN TEXAS

Armstrong, W.E., and E.L. Young. 2000. White-tailed Deer management in the Texas Hill Country. PWD RP W7000-0828. Texas Parks and Wildlife Department. 53 pp.

Baccus, J.T. 2002. Impacts of game ranching on wildlife management in Texas. Transactions of the North American Wildlife and Natural Resources Conference 67:276–288.

Bolen, E.G., and W.L. Robinson. 2003. Wildlife ecology and management. 5th ed. Prentice Hall, Upper Saddle River, NJ. 634 pp.

Butler, L.D. 1991. White-tailed Deer hunting leases: Hunter costs and rancher revenues. Rangelands 13:20–22.

Butler, M.J., A.P. Teaschner, W.B. Ballard, and B.K. McGee. 2005. Commentary: Wildlife ranching in North America—arguments, issues, and perspectives. Wildlife Society Bulletin 33:381–389.

Faas, C.J., and F.W. Weckerly. 2010. Habitat interference by Axis Deer on White-tailed Deer. Journal of Wildlife Management 74:698–706.

Henke, D.E., S. Demarais, and J.A. Pfister. 1988. Digestive capacity and diets of White-tailed Deer and exotic ruminants. Journal of Wildlife Management 52:595–598.

Mungall, C. 2000. Exotics. Pp. 736–764 *in* Ecology and management of large mammals in North America (S. Demarais and P.R. Krausman, eds.). Prentice Hall, Upper Saddle River, NJ. 778 pp.

Richardson, M.L., and S. Demarais. 1992. Parasites and condition of coexisting White-tailed Deer and exotic deer in south-central Texas. Journal of Wildlife Diseases 28:485–489.

Teer, J.G. 1975. Commercial uses of game animals on rangelands of Texas. Journal of Animal Science 40:1000–1008.

The Wildlife Society. 2009. Final position statement: Confinement of wild ungulates within high fences. The Wildlife Society, Bethesda, MD. 2 pp.

Conservation and Management

Allen, C.R., S. Demarais, and R.S. Lutz. 1994. Red Imported Fire Ant impact on wildlife: An overview. Texas Journal of Science 46:51–60.

Burkalova, L.E., A.Y. Karateyev, V.A. Karatayev, et al. 2011. Biogeography and conservation of freshwater mussels (Bivalvia: Unionidae) in Texas: Patterns of diversity and threats. Diversity and Distributions 17:393–407.

Fowler, N.L., and D.W. Dunlap. 1986. Grassland vegetation of the eastern Edwards Plateau. American Midland Naturalist 115:146–155.

Howells, R.G., R.W. Neck, and H.D. Murray. 1996. Freshwater mussels of Texas. Texas Parks and Wildlife Department, Austin. 218 pp.

Mabe, J.A., and J. Kennedy. 2014. Habitat conditions associated with a reproducing population of the critically endangered freshwater mussel *Quadrula mitchelli* in

Central Texas. Southwestern Naturalist 59:297–300.

Pool, W.C. 1975. A historical atlas of Texas. Encino Press, Austin, TX. 190 pp.

Smeins, F.E., and L.B. Merrill. 1988. Long-term change in a semiarid grassland. Pp. 101–104 *in* Edwards Plateau vegetation: Plant ecological studies in Central Texas (B.B. Amos and F.R. Gehlbach, eds.). Baylor University Press, Waco, TX. 144 pp.

Texas Water Commission. 1989. Ground water quality of Texas—An overview of natural and man-affected conditions. Texas Water Commission Report 89–01. 197 pp.

Infobox 5. Texas Wildflowers—Lady Bird's Legacy

Gillette, M.L. 2012. Lady Bird Johnson: An oral history. Oxford University Press, New York. 416 pp.

Gould, L.L. 1999. Lady Bird Johnson: Our environmental First Lady. University Press of Kansas, Lawrence. 176 pp.

Johnson, L.B., and C.B. Lees. 1998. Wildflowers across America. Abbeville Press, New York. 312 pp.

Paulson, A. 1989. The National Wildflower Research Center handbook. Texas Monthly Press, Austin. 337 pp.

Infobox 6. Living Sponges in Texas Rivers?

Anakina, R.P. 2010. Sponges as biological indicators and remedial components of freshwater ecological systems. Biosphere 2:397–408.

Davis, J.R. 1980a. Species composition and diversity of benthic macroinvertebrate populations of the Pecos River, Texas. Southwestern Naturalist 25:241–256.

———. 1980b. Species composition and diversity of benthic

macroinvertebrates of lower Devil's River, Texas. Southwestern Naturalist 25:379–384.

Nichols, H.T., and T.H. Bonner. 2014. First record and habitat associations of *Spongilla cenota* (Class Demospongiae) within streams of the Edwards Plateau, Texas, USA. Southwestern Naturalist 59:467–472.

Porrier, M.A. 1969. Fresh-water sponge hosts of Louisiana and Texas spongilla-flies, with new locality records. American Midland Naturalist 81:573–575.

———. 1972. Additional records of Texas fresh-water sponges (Spongillidae) with the first record of *Radiospongilla cerebellata* (Bowerbank, 1863) from the Western Hemisphere. Southwestern Naturalist 16:434–435.

Reiswig, H., T.M. Frost, and A. Ricciardi. 2010. Porifera. Pp. 91–123 *in* Ecology and classification of North American freshwater invertebrates (J. Thorp and A. Covich, eds.). Elsevier, Oxford, UK. 1021 pp.

Infobox 7. Guano, Gunpowder, and Bat Bombs

Campbell, R.B. 2003. Gone to Texas: A history of the Lone Star State. Oxford University Press, New York. 265 pp.

Constantine, D.G. 1957. Color variation and molt in *Tadarida brasiliensis* and *Myotis velifer*. Journal of Mammalogy 38:461–466.

———. 1958. Bleaching of hair pigment of bats by the atmosphere in caves. Journal of Mammalogy 39:513–520.

Couffer, J. 1992. Bat bomb: World War II's other secret weapon. University of Texas Press, Austin. 252 pp.

Davis, R.B., C.F. Herrid II, and H.L. Short. 1962. Mexican Free-tailed Bats in Texas. Ecological Monographs 32:311–346.

Mohr, C.E. 1948. Texas bat caves served in three wars. National Speleological Bulletin 10:89–96.

Infobox 8. Clark Hubbs (1921–2008): Ichthyologist and Eminent Naturalist

Holtcamp, W. 2011. Legend, lore and legacy: The fish wrangler. Texas Parks and Wildlife Magazine (April).

Marsh-Matthews, E. 2008. Clark Hubbs: 1921–2008. Southwestern Naturalist 53:539–541.

Martin, F.D., R.J. Edwards, D.A. Hendrickson, and G.P. Garrett. 2008. Obituary: Clark Hubbs, 1921–2008, Ichthyologist. Fisheries 33:302.

Matthews, R. 2008. Dr. Clark Hubbs: March 15, 1921–February 3, 2008. Texas Academy of Science, 11th Annual Meeting Program and Abstracts 2008:14–15.

Infobox 9. The Nature of Roy Bedichek (1878–1959)

Bedichek, R. 1947. Adventures with a Texas naturalist. Doubleday, Garden City, NY. 293 pp.

———. 1950. Karankaway Country. Doubleday, Garden City, NY. 290 pp.

Dugger, R., ed. 1967. Three men in Texas: Bedichek, Webb, and Dobie. University of Texas Press, Austin. 285 pp.

Owens, W.A., and L. Grant, eds. 1985. The letters of Roy Bedichek. University of Texas Press, Austin. 542 pp.

Walker, S. 1948. The lively hermit of Friday Mountain. Saturday Evening Post, October 16. Pp. 38–39, 57–58, 61.

INDEX

Note: Page numbers in *italics* denote illustrations.